CAMPAIGN 416

CYNOSCEPHALAE 197 BC

Rome Humbles Macedon

MARK VAN DER ENDEN   ILLUSTRATED BY MARCO CAPPARONI

OSPREY PUBLISHING
Bloomsbury Publishing Plc
Kemp House, Chawley Park, Cumnor Hill, Oxford OX2 9PH, UK
Bloomsbury Publishing Ireland Limited,
29 Earlsfort Terrace, Dublin 2, D02 AY28, Ireland
1385 Broadway, 5th Floor, New York, NY 10018, USA
E-mail: info@ospreypublishing.com
www.ospreypublishing.com

OSPREY is a trademark of Osprey Publishing Ltd

First published in Great Britain in 2025

© Osprey Publishing Ltd, 2025

All rights reserved. No part of this publication may be: i) reproduced or transmitted in any form, electronic or mechanical, including photocopying, recording or by means of any information storage or retrieval system without prior permission in writing from the publishers; or ii) used or reproduced in any way for the training, development or operation of artificial intelligence (AI) technologies, including generative AI technologies. The rights holders expressly reserve this publication from the text and data mining exception as per Article 4(3) of the Digital Single Market Directive (EU) 2019/790

A catalogue record for this book is available from the British Library.

ISBN: PB 9781472865380; eBook 9781472865403; ePDF 9781472865397; XML 9781472865410

25 26 27 28 29   10 9 8 7 6 5 4 3 2 1

Maps by Bounford.com
3D BEVs by Paul Kime
Index by Fionbar Lyons
Typeset by PDQ Digital Media Solutions, Bungay, UK
Printed by Repro India Ltd

Osprey Publishing supports the Woodland Trust, the UK's leading woodland conservation charity.

To find out more about our authors and books visit www.ospreypublishing.com. Here you will find extracts, author interviews, details of forthcoming events and the option to sign up for our newsletter.

For product safety related questions contact productsafety@bloomsbury.com

Dedication

To Salem, with whom I spent a last summer together reading in the garden about Philip V. You are greatly missed.

Acknowledgements

This work has benefited from the generous support, guidance and encouragement of numerous individuals. First and foremost, I would like to express my utmost thanks to the editorial team at Osprey. The encouragement, support, guidance and patience of Nikolai Bogdanovic, Brianne Bellio and Alexandra Boulton has been tremendously appreciated. I would also like to express my heartfelt thanks to Peter Dennis for encouraging me to try and write an Osprey Campaign title in the first place.

I am very grateful to Professor Jake Morton who kindly talked me through his research and generously allowed me to draw on his cartographic material. The 2D maps in this work are based upon his excellent study of the movements of the combatants during the various campaigns of the war. I am very indebted also to Professors Mathhew Sears and Jake Butera. They very generously provided me with photographic material of the battlefield area and talked me through their ideas about the battle. Matthew also very kindly reviewed sections of the work and his advice and support have been tremendously appreciated. I am equally grateful to Dr Robin Waterfield for sharing and allowing me to use his photos of the Cynoscephalae battlefield and Myke Cole for his advice and encouragement. Professor Vladimir Stissi also very generously shared his extensive knowledge of Thessaly and patiently answered my various questions. I would also like to express my utmost thanks to Dr Daniel Stewart and Dr Charlotte van Regenmortel for reviewing drafts of the book.

Finally, I would like to express my thanks and love to my partner Estefania and cats Nella and Ares, who patiently put up with me talking incessantly about spurs and hilltops, providing unwavering encouragement and support throughout the process of writing this book.

Front cover main illustration: Philip's narrow escape. (Marco Capparoni)
Title page photograph: The advance of the Macedonian right wing at the battle of Cynoscephalae. (Elbert Perce, public domain, via Wikimedia Commons)

CONTENTS

ORIGINS OF THE CAMPAIGN	5
CHRONOLOGY	15
OPPOSING COMMANDERS	16
The Roman Republic ▪ Antigonid Macedon	
OPPOSING FORCES	20
The Roman Republic ▪ Antigonid Macedon ▪ Orders of battle	
OPPOSING PLANS	33
The Roman Republic ▪ Antigonid Macedon	
THE CAMPAIGN	35
Opening moves ▪ Sulpicius' assault on Western Macedonia ▪ The Battle for the Aous gorge ▪ The Cynoscephalae campaign	
AFTERMATH	88
THE BATTLEFIELD TODAY	91
BIBLIOGRAPHY	92
INDEX	95

Overview of the Hellenistic Aegean

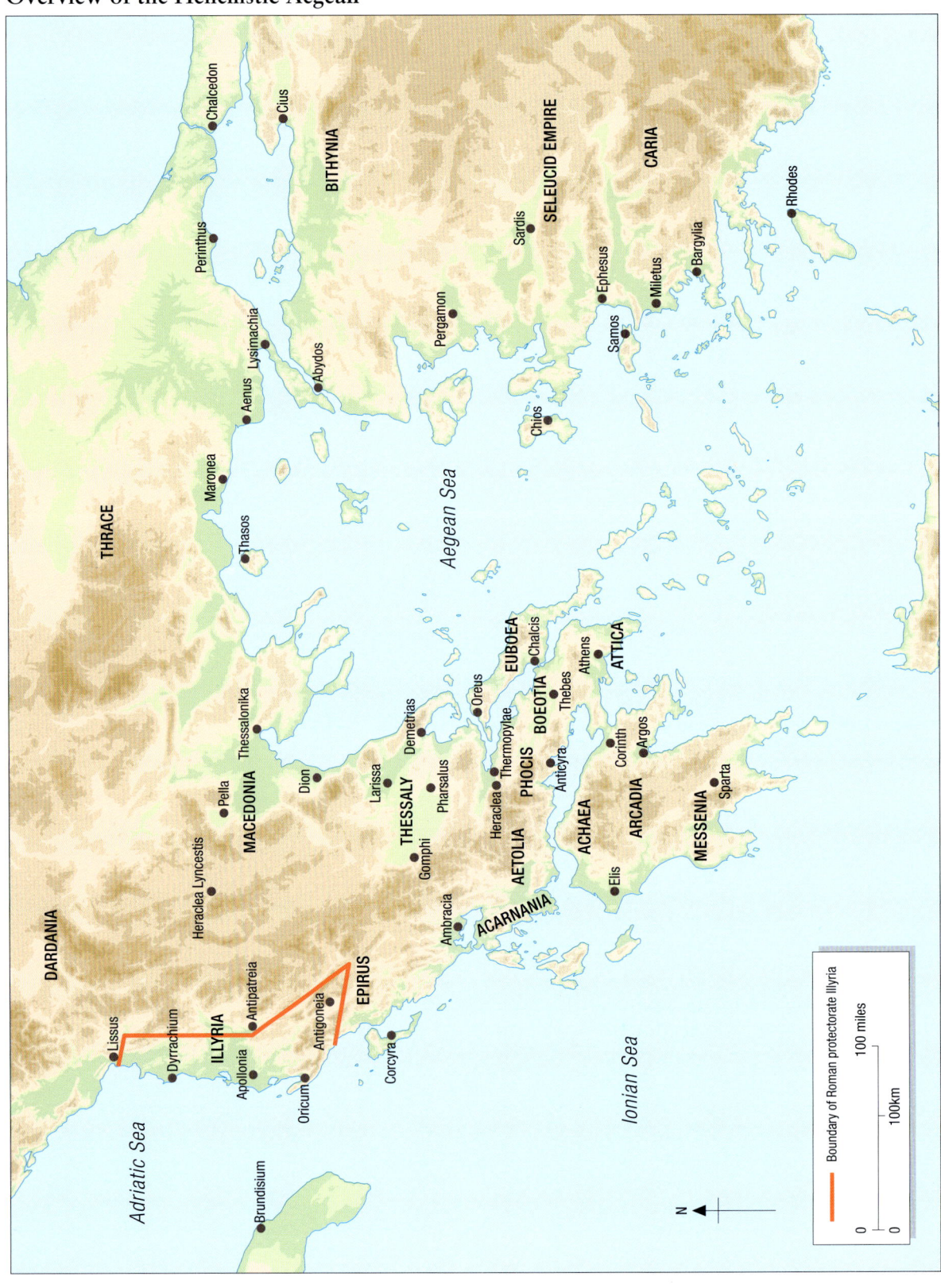

ORIGINS OF THE CAMPAIGN

When Alexander the Great died in Babylon in 323 BC, the short-lived Empire he had created, which ranged from the shores of Greece to the Indian subcontinent, started to fall apart. His surviving generals squabbled among themselves for control of the Empire and started to carve out their own territories. The murder in 310 BC of Alexander's young son saw the extinction of the Argead royal line, which opened the door for Alexander's former generals to claim royal status for themselves; the first to do so was Antigonus Monophthalmos (meaning 'one-eyed'), quickly followed by the others. More fighting ensued and eventually, one by one, the various contenders were whittled down until, in the end, only three major new royal dynasties achieved a permanent footing in the new geo-political constellation of the post-Alexandrian Eastern Mediterranean. The descendants of Alexander's friend and companion Ptolemy would rule Egypt until the death of Cleopatra VII in 30 BC. The offspring of Seleukos, former commander of the *hypaspistai*, Alexander's elite multi-purpose infantry unit, ruled most of Asia Minor and the heartlands of the former Persian Empire until Pompey the Great did away with the dynasty in 64 BC with the creation of the Roman province of Syria. In Macedon itself, the Antigonids, descendants of Antigonus Monophthalmos, who had once aspired to regaining control of the whole of Alexander's Empire, ruled. They would continue to dominate the affairs of Greece for the next 80 years. It was the coming of Rome, however, that would upend this threefold division and ultimately abolish almost three centuries of Macedonian domination of the Hellenistic East. The Greek historian Polybius, whose works together with the writings of Titus Livius form our principal sources for the period under study, referred to this process as *symploke*, an intertwining or coming together of the geo-politics of the Western and Eastern Mediterranean. All this,

The death of Alexander as depicted in the *Shahnama*, the Persian book of kings. The great conqueror of the Persian Empire left no ready heir to rule over his dominions, only a pregnant queen. As a result, his former generals divided up his empire and created their own royal dynasties. (Album/Alamy Stock Photo)

however, originated in 229 BC. It was in this year that the Romans crossed the Adriatic in force for the first time and, in so doing, unknowingly set in motion a series of events that would first challenge and then overturn the geo-political dominance of the Greco-Macedonian successor kingdoms. At Cynoscephalae in 197 BC, the legions would for the first time defeat the vaunted Macedonian phalanx on its home turf, establishing not only the superiority of the Roman way of making war but also breaking Macedon's traditional dominance over the affairs of Greece.

Flashpoint Illyria

The rationale behind Rome's unprecedented intervention across the Adriatic was to be found in Illyria. The area, encompassing what is now modern Albania and Croatia, was home to various tribes who had recently coalesced into a more or less unified Illyrian kingdom. Under King Agron and, after his death, his widow Teuta, the Illyrians had adopted a policy of expansion and state-sponsored raiding. Its primary victims were nearby Epirus and the shores of Elis and Messenia on the western Peloponnese, but Italian traders had also fallen victim to the depravations of Illyrian privateers. It was their complaints that caused the Roman Republic to furrow its metaphorical brow and demand a stop to such outrages. Ambassadors were dispatched to Teuta but received a less than satisfactory response (with one ambassador being assassinated on the way home reportedly in retaliation for insulting the queen).

The Roman response was not long in coming and arrived in the form of the armed punitive expedition. Teuta had overplayed her hand; her forces were no match for the Roman legionaries and were quickly defeated in what became known as the First Illyrian War (229 BC) (Polyb.2.8). The result of this brief conflict was the Roman Republic establishing a protectorate on the shores of Illyria encompassing a number of Greek cities including Corcyra, Apollonia and Epidamnus (Polyb.2.11). Demetrius of Pharos, a former henchman of Teuta who had come over to the Romans, became the new dominant political figure in Illyria with Roman support. Ten years later, it became apparent that Rome was determined to uphold and defend its interests in the area. Demetrius of Pharos had used his time in charge well, extending his power and influence. He had also returned to the traditional Illyrian pastime of state-sponsored raiding. Rome responded by sending its armed forces across the Adriatic for a second time. The subsequent Second Illyrian War (219 BC) was equally short. Two key Illyrian fortresses were quickly taken, tribal unity collapsed and Demetrius was forced to flee, making his way to Macedon (Polyb.3.16–19).

Teuta was an Illyrian queen and regent for her young son. Unwilling to curb the piratical exploits of her subjects in the Adriatic, she ran afoul of the Roman Republic, triggering unprecedented Roman intervention across the Adriatic after further territorial aggression and the murder of a Roman envoy. (Augustyn Mirys, public domain, via Wikimedia Commons)

Macedon and Greece

In 219 BC, Macedon was ruled by Philip V, grandson of Antigonus II Gonatas, the king who finally secured the Antigonid hold over Macedonia. Philip, 19 years of age, had been on the throne since 221 BC. He was not only

The ruined remains of Apollonia. Visible is the temple of Diana, built during the last quarter of the 2nd century BC. Founded in 600 BC, Apollonia was a strategically located Greek city in Illyria. Situated near the mouth of the River Aous, it received the attentions of Philip V on multiple occasions. (Pudelek, CC BY-SA 4.0 https://creativecommons.org/licenses/by-sa/4.0, via Wikimedia Commons)

king of the Macedonians but also headed up the Hellenic Security Pact, an organization created by his immediate predecessor Antigonus III Doson. The pact formally united Macedon in alliance with the federal leagues of Thessaly, Epirus, Acarnania, Boeotia, Phocis and Achaea. Macedonian control over the affairs of Greece was further facilitated by having established garrisons in what were called the 'fetters' of Greece, referring to the fortress cities of Demetrias in Thessaly, Chalcis on the island of Euboea and the citadel at Acrocorinth on the isthmus of Corinth. Together these strongpoints enabled the Macedonian king to move his army south into central Greece (bypassing the traditional chokepoint at Thermopylae by going via Chalcis) and gain access to the Peloponnese.

In 219 BC, when Demetrius of Pharos arrived at the Antigonid court, Philip and his allies were engaged in the Social War (220–217 BC), fighting the Aetolians and their allies. The Aetolian league was centred on west–central Greece and played, as we will see, a pivotal role in the events covered in this study. During the 3rd century BC, the Aetolians were able to expand their power, gaining control over Delphi and enrolling communities in Thrace, Asia Minor and the Black Sea area as members of their league. Like the

The ruins of Ancient Corinth with the temple of Apollo in the foreground. Hovering over the city is the acropolis, Acrocorinth. As one of the 'fetters' of Greece, control of this fortress enabled Macedon to dominate the access route to the Peloponnese. (George E. Koronaios, CC BY-SA 4.0 https://creativecommons.org/licenses/by-sa/4.0, via Wikimedia Commons)

Illyrians, the Aetolians were notorious for regularly raiding their neighbours. Epirus and Achaea suffered in particular, and as members of the Hellenic Security Pact, they appealed to Philip for help. The resulting war would last for three years and saw the young Macedonian king energetically campaigning across Greece, leading his men through numerous engagements and establishing a reputation for hard marching and military competency. After much fighting and destruction, peace was signed in 217 BC, basically confirming the status quo with each side holding on to the territory currently under their control.

Back to Illyria

According to Polybius, Philip's desire to end the war with Aetolia can be ascribed to the influence of Demetrius of Pharos, who after his flight from Illyria had become an advisor to the young king. Wishing to recover his former position, Demetrius would have encouraged Philip to take advantage of Rome's current struggles and intervene in Illyria. Since 218 BC, the Romans had been at war

Painting in the royal palace in Amsterdam by Ferdinand Bol (1616–80). It depicts the Epirote King Pyrrhus negotiating with the Roman consul Fabritius. Philip V was accused, most likely falsely, of wanting to emulate Pyrrhus and invade Italy himself. (Historic Images/Alamy Stock Photo)

with Hannibal's Carthage, and to say that things had not gone well for the Republic is a bit of an understatement. First there had been the defeat at Trasimene (217 BC), followed by the disaster at Cannae (216 BC). Rome appeared thoroughly occupied by the war with Carthage and was unlikely to be willing or able to pay much attention to events in Illyria. Polybius even credits Philip with having designs on Italy itself and, wanting to get in on the action, using Illyria as a stepping stone for a cross-Adriatic invasion in the mould of Pyrrhus of Epirus. In reality, however, Philip's interest in Illyria had less to do with Rome than with Macedon's traditional security concerns. A recent Illyrian raid on Upper Macedonia required an adequate response and provided the rationale for further securing the western approaches to the kingdom (Polyb.5.108). In preparation for his punitive expedition against the Illyrian chieftain responsible for the raid, Philip ordered the construction of a fleet of 100 *lembi*, smaller highly manoeuvrable vessels suitable for raiding, during the winter of 216 BC. The Macedonian expedition, however, ended in farce with nothing achieved. When learning of the imminent arrival of the Macedonian fleet, the Illyrians had appealed to Rome for help and the mere rumour of a Roman fleet at sea and on its way was enough for Philip to abandon his plans and immediately reverse course.

The First Macedonian War

Philip now committed what, in retrospect, would be his greatest mistake. In 214 BC, it was by no means clear that the Roman Republic would be able to stave off defeat, and a Carthaginian victory seemed entirely possible. Philip thus reasoned (again possibly urged on by Demetrius) that an alliance with Carthage would be to Macedon's benefit. Ambassadors were dispatched to make this happen but, unfortunately for the king, the draft treaty fell into Roman hands, making them aware of the king's designs. Outraged by this perceived and unsolicited stab in the back during their time of greatest need, the Romans were determined to keep the Macedonians out of Illyria and made their military dispositions accordingly: a Roman fleet under Marcus Valerius Laevinus was dispatched to Illyrian waters.

With the cat out of the bag, Philip decided to repeat his attempt of 216 BC and readied his fleet, again consisting of *lembi*, for another descent upon Illyria, targeting the key city of Apollonia. Still keen to avoid a confrontation with the Roman fleet, Philip moved when he received intelligence that the latter was away in Sicilian waters (Polyb.5.109). The king took his fleet up the River Aous and put Apollonia – which is located inland further up the river – under siege. Unbeknown to him, however, Laevinus and the Roman fleet arrived, blocked off the mouth of the River Aous and sent a contingent of 2,000 men under cover of darkness into the besieged city. Macedonian camp discipline was lax and, the next evening, the Romans launched an attack upon the unsuspecting Macedonians, which overran their camp. Leaving 3,000 dead and at least as many prisoners behind, the king retreated with the survivors over land to Macedonia, having burnt his fleet after realizing it was now trapped by the more powerful Roman navy awaiting him at the mouth of the river (Liv.24.40). The whole expedition, therefore, was an unmitigated disaster for the Macedonian king. Philip did not give up, however, and was back in action the next year, invading Illyria overland from Macedonia. This time, he was able to establish his control over most of Illyria, reducing the Roman zone of control to the coastal areas around Dyrrachium, Apollonia and Oricum.

In response to these new developments, the Romans looked around for allies. Because of the ongoing struggle with Carthage in Italy, the senate was unwilling to commit large numbers of troops to the Illyrian theatre. From Rome's perspective, the conflict would ideally be fought mostly by proxy. Laevinus, therefore, set himself the task of convincing the Aetolians to join the fight on the side of Rome, which they officially did in 211 BC (Liv.26.24).

Events had thus quickly spiralled out of control for Philip and Macedon. Having most likely envisioned a limited conflict confined to Illyria, the king now found himself embroiled in an ever-widening war on multiple fronts. The entry of Aetolia into the war expanded the fighting into Thessaly and Acarnania (Liv.26.25; Polyb.9.40), and when Sparta, Messenia and Elis joined the Roman alliance, Philip's Achaean allies on the Peloponnese were directly threatened. A further threat was added when King Attalus I of Pergamon involved himself in the situation (Liv.27.29). If that was not enough, a Macedonian king always needed to keep one wary eye directed northwards where Dardanians and Thracians stood ready to take advantage of any perceived weakness to spill across the borders of Macedon.

An Illyrian coin depicting a *lembos* with its characteristic prow. *Lembi* were agile, fast-moving ships ideally suited to the raiding activities of the Illyrians. Philip V commissioned a fleet of these vessels for his descent on Apollonia. (Hyjnesha, CC BY-SA 4.0 https://creativecommons.org/licenses/by-sa/4.0, via Wikimedia Commons)

Coin of Antigonus II Gonatas, grandfather of Philip V. He re-established the power of Macedon after the upheavals of the wars of the successors. It was Antigonus who finally secured Antigonid rule over Macedon, securing the throne for his descendants. (Classical Numismatic Group, Inc. http://www.cngcoins.com, CC BY-SA 2.5 https://creativecommons.org/licenses/by-sa/2.5, via Wikimedia Commons)

The Romans, in due course, joined by the Pergamenes, restricted themselves to naval operations, attacking coastal towns garrisoned by Macedon (Liv.26.26). Philip, however, almost succeeded in knocking Aetolia out of the war in 209 BC, defeating them and their Roman allies decisively in two battles near Lamia in Thessaly (Liv.27.30). Operations then moved to the area of Corinth and the Peloponnese. A subsequent battle fought at Elis followed in which the Macedonian king charged the Roman contingent supporting the Aetolians at the head of his cavalry. The Macedonians were defeated, however, and Philip narrowly made his escape after being thrown off his horse in the heat of battle. The new year, 208 BC, saw Macedon embattled on all sides with its allies petitioning the king for support and protection. Philip promised help and support to all, disposed his troops as best he could and kept the field army at the ready (Polyb.10.41; Liv.28.6) to respond to the movements and incursions of his enemies.

Their next blow fell on Oreus, a key defensive strongpoint on the island of Euboea, which was treacherously surrendered to the Roman fleet by its governor. Chalcis, one of the 'fetters' of Greece, was next in line. The Romans and their allies failed, however, to take the town. Not long after, the Attalid king learned that the territory of Pergamon itself was being invaded by the neighbouring kingdom of Bithynia (coincidently ruled by Philip's brother-in-law) and he decided to call it a day, returning to Asia (Liv.28.8). With Attalus out of the fight, the Aetolians' will to continue the struggle was beginning to waver. They felt Roman support had been lacking, because, apart from the Roman fleet, no significant land forces had been committed to the Greek theatre for about two years. Naturally, Rome was greatly distracted by the war with Hannibal Barca and attempted to fight the Macedonian war with minimal resources (Liv.26.28). The Aetolians, therefore, made their peace with Philip in 206 BC, leaving the Romans to their own devices. Bereft of allies, the Romans came to terms with Philip a year later, bringing the First Macedonian War to an end.

A brief respite/interlude

The war had been a qualified success for the Macedonian king. Philip had been able to ward off the attacks of his enemies and, by and large, successfully defended his allies in Greece. The peace had confirmed this and provided Macedon with some territorial gains. Rome, however, had retained its foothold in Illyria (Liv.29.12). Philip V now shifted his focus to Thrace, an area controlled by Macedon in the time of Philip II. In 203 BC, he also concluded a secret pact or alliance with Antiochus III of the Seleucid Empire, allegedly created to divvy up the possessions of the failing Ptolemaic kingdom among themselves (Polyb.15.20; Liv.13.14.5; Just.30.2.8). It has been argued, however, that Philip's actions in the Aegean and the infamous pact (which remained secret and for the moment was not acted upon) need to be seen as defensive measures to safeguard traditional Macedonian interests, such as securing the grain supply coming from the Black Sea.

Militarily, Philip was highly successful, taking in quick succession the cities of Lysimachia, Chalcedon, Perinthus, Cius and Thasos. These activities, however, involved the razing and enslaving of communities, upsetting in particular Aetolia (to whose league several of the cities targeted had enrolled) and Rhodes, but also appalling the wider Greek world (Polyb.15.23–24). A direct consequence of these developments, apart from the enmity of

Rhodes and Aetolia, was the latter seeking Roman assistance against Macedon. Rome, though, was not interested. The Republic appeared not to have been overly concerned by the recent Macedonian aggressions and was in any case gearing up for the final showdown with Hannibal. The Aetolian entreaties were rebuffed (Liv.31.29.4; App. Mac.4.2). The Aetolian appeal, however, did appear to spur Philip on into taking decisive action against Rhodes, possibly in an attempt to knock Rhodes out of any potential future conflict with Rome.

At this stage, Philip had cobbled together a new fleet, and unlike with his earlier maritime endeavours, this fleet consisted of proper men of war suitable to stand up to the rigours of a sea battle. Taking this fleet to the island of Samos, which he used as a base of operations, Philip was now operating in Rhodian home waters. At Lade, near Miletus, the Rhodian fleet sailed to stop him, but it was put to flight surrendering two *quinqueremes* (large warships) in the process (Polyb.16.10; 16.15). The Macedonians then proceeded to gain control of Miletus and invaded Caria, taking over Rhodian possessions on the mainland (Polyb.16.11–12). The Rhodian defeat and subsequent Macedonian naval supremacy greatly concerned Attalus I of Pergamon, who decided to prop up the failing Rhodians. Having combined their forces, the Rhodians and Pergamenes sought to strike back, so a major sea battle was fought near Chios. Polybius provides a detailed description of the action and numbers involved. Philip had at his disposal 53 large warships consisting of *quadriremes* and *quinquiremes*. This main strike force was supported by 150 *lembi*. Overall, the king commanded a force of around 30,000 men. He was opposed by 65 large Rhodian and Pergamene warships plus supporting

Head identified as Antiochus III, nicknamed the Great, king of the Seleucid Empire, now in the Louvre. Note the diadem, a symbol of Macedonian royal status. It was Philip's pact with Antiochus, which, when known, caused alarm in the Aegean and helped to trigger the Roman intervention in Greece. (Carole Raddato from FRANKFURT, Germany, CC BY-SA 2.0 https://creativecommons.org/licenses/by-sa/2.0, via Wikimedia Commons)

Relief of Rhodian *trireme* carved into the rock at Lindos and dated to 180 BC. Rhodes was a significant naval power during the Hellenistic period and together with Pergamon had challenged Macedonian naval activities in the Aegean. These activities would ultimately lead to the outbreak of a renewed war with Rome. (Saffron Blaze, CC BY-SA 3.0 https://creativecommons.org/licenses/by-sa/3.0, via Wikimedia Commons)

The acropolis of Pergamon with the temple of Trajan in the foreground. Pergamon was a medium-sized independent kingdom during the Hellenistic period. Its rulers were keen to maintain their independence and expand their own influence in the face of Seleucid and Macedonian pressure. (Ferit BAYCUMAN, CC BY-SA 4.0 https://creativecommons.org/licenses/by-sa/4.0, via Wikimedia Commons)

vessels (Polyb.16.2). The ensuing battle was hard fought and, in the end, the Rhodian and Pergamene navies withdrew, allowing the Macedonians to claim victory. In victory, however, Philip had tasted defeat. His losses were severe; 28 of his large ships and around 75 *lembi* were destroyed, and 9,000 soldiers and sailors perished. A further two ships and 3,000 men were captured, losses on a truly devastating scale if reported correctly. The fact that Pergamene and Rhodian losses amounted to a mere nine ships lost and three captured with the loss of only 130 men points, however, to a likely exaggeration of Macedonian casualties (Polyb.16.7).

Despite claiming victory, subsequent developments do indicate that the battle had cost the Macedonians the ability to contest the waves against the combined forces of the Rhodians and Pergamenes. Philip, however, was undeterred; just as in Illyria during 214 BC when forced to burn his own fleet, he now decided to make an attempt overland, marching his army to the gates of Pergamon. The Macedonians, however, proved unable to take the city due to its strong defences and were restricted to ravishing the countryside in frustration before beating an ignominious retreat (Polyb.16.1). Philip was unable to sustain his campaign due to a lack of supplies, and now his inability to maintain naval superiority over his opponents made itself felt. Running out of supplies and with the remainder of his fleet blockaded by the combined Rhodian and Pergamene navies at Bargylia, Philip was fast running out of options and was forced to raid the surrounding area for provisions and rely on limited Seleucid help (Polyb.16.24). The situation was unsustainable and after a number of months, in the spring of 200 BC, Philip decided to cut his losses and break out of the blockade using a ruse to throw the Pergamenes and Rhodians off his scent (Polyaenus.Strat.IV.18.2; Liv.31.14.11; Polyb.16.24).

The conflict escalates

Developments now took a very interesting and much debated turn. Pergamon and Rhodes had successfully seen off Philip, whose naval ambitions in the Aegean had been thwarted. Although able to escape back home to Macedon, Philip's Aegean endeavours had been a costly enterprise, the defeat at Chios, if reported casualties can be taken at face value, ranking as his greatest defeat. Why then, with the situation in hand, did Pergamon and Rhodes decide to appeal to Rome for help and seek the Republic's intervention in what appeared to be a localized spat between rival Aegean powers? MacDonald and Walbank (1937:187) have argued that it was then, during the summer of 201 BC, that Macedon's secret pact with the Seleucid Empire of Antiochus III was discovered. Both Pergamon and Rhodes when learning of this, in their eyes, unholy alliance, immediately identified its existence as an existential threat to the status quo in the Aegean. Envoys were sent off to Rome to enlist the Republic's support in countering the perceived threat.

Rome's response to the entreaties of Pergamon and Rhodes (Liv.31.2.1–2) was to investigate the matter. For this purpose, ambassadors were sent out to Greece. It appears that the senate at this stage was leaning towards renewing the war with Macedon. Why this sudden eagerness to reopen hostilities? Various suggestions have been made. It seems to a certain extent that Rome considered Philip unfinished business. The First Macedonian War from a Roman perspective had had an unsatisfactory ending, and the feeling that Philip had engaged in hostilities with Rome both unprovoked and during the hour of its greatest need was real enough. Reports that Macedonian soldiers fought with Hannibal at Zama, true or not, will have added fuel to the fire (Liv.31.1.9). An exaggerated perception of the threat posed by Macedon, fuelled by the memories of Rome's experience with Pyrrhus, undoubtedly also played a role. Furthermore, as the war with Carthage had come to an end, the martial aspirations of the Roman elite needed a new outlet. All these factors appear to have combined in creating a political climate in which military intervention east of the Adriatic would not be dismissed out of hand. What appears, however, to have been the trigger to Rome's decision to actively seek war was the news brought by Pergamon and Rhodes, however exaggerated, of the Macedonian–Seleucid pact. It seems that Philip's naval aspirations in the Aegean combined with allying himself with Antiochus III had alarmed Rome sufficiently enough to the extent that it was willing to act.

Philip had become embroiled in another conflict at around the same time, this time with the city of Athens. The latter had put to death two Acarnanians. The Acarnanian League sought redress, and as a member of the Hellenic Security Pact turned to Philip for support, who instructed his generals to raid Attica (Liv.31.14.6–8). Philip now found himself at war not only with Pergamon and Rhodes but also Athens. All of this coincided with the Roman ambassadors reaching Greece and Athens. It was at the latter

A Macedonian coin with a helmet on the reverse. Coins such as these provide insights into the types of helmets used by the Macedonian army under the Antigonids. Here we see a brimmed *pilos* or *konos* with crest. (Public domain, CC0, via Wikimedia Commons)

An example from Side (Türkiye) of Hellenistic helmets and linen corselets. The crested helmets are of the conical *pilos* or *konos* variety and adorned with crest and cheek guards. Note the ornamental visor. (Ad Meskens, CC BY-SA 3.0 https://creativecommons.org/licenses/by-sa/3.0, via Wikimedia Commons)

city that Philip's general Nicanor was handed an ultimatum (Polyb.16.27; 27.2–3): Macedon was to stop making war on the Greeks and compensate Attalus for damages sustained during Philip's attack on Pergamon or face war. The Romans stopped short of declaring war, however, as the Roman popular assembly had rejected, for the moment, a motion to declare war on Macedon (Liv.31.6.1–6; App. Mac.4.2; Just.30.3). War weariness seemed to lie behind this decision. The Roman message, duly passed on by Nicanor to his king, was ignored by Philip.

The king of the Macedonians proceeded to campaign in Thrace and on the Chersonese, focusing this time on Ptolemaic possessions. His forces took several places including Maronea and Aenus, and laid siege to Abydos (Liv.31.14.6; 31.15.16), which is where one of the Roman ambassadors, Marcus Aemilius Lepidus, caught up with the king. By then, a second attempt at shepherding a declaration of war through the Roman popular assembly had succeeded and Lepidus, upon receiving this news, was authorized to deliver a formal declaration of war (Liv.7.6.7). Lepidus accused Philip of attacking Attalus and Rhodes, and urged him to stop attacking Ptolemaic possessions. Philip's reply was that he had not broken the peace and instead accused Rhodes and Pergamon of unprovoked aggression. He added he did not seek war with Rome, but was ready to defend himself if attacked (Liv.31.18). The Roman response was uncompromising: Philip was to stop making war on the Greeks, and failing to do so would result in war. Rejecting this notion, Philip pressed on with the siege of Abydos. The Roman ambassadors continued on to pay a visit to Antiochus III, verifying the great king had no intentions to join in the coming conflict (Liv.33.20.8). Thus, the stage was set for the second war between the Romans and the Macedonians. As Philip arrived back home in Macedon, after successfully completing the siege of Abydos, he learned that the legions were already on their way, having landed in Apollonia (Liv.31.18.9).

CHRONOLOGY[1]

229 BC	Rome's First Illyrian War.	200 BC	
221 BC	Philip V becomes king of Macedon.	September–October	Raid by Apustius; capture of Antipatreia.
219 BC	Second Illyrian War and start of the Social War.	October	Roman attack on Chalcis.
218 BC	Start of the Second Punic War and the battle of Trebia.	October–November	Macedonian attacks on Athens.
217 BC	Battle of Lake Trasimene and the end of the Social War.	199 BC	
216 BC	Philip's first attempt on Illyria by sea.	May–June	Advance of Galba via Genusus valley; skirmishes between Roman and Macedonian forces.
214 BC	Philip attempts to capture Apollonia, and is forced to burn his fleet; start of the First Macedonian War.	July	Macedonian defeat at Otolobus.
		September	Aetolia joins Rome and invades Thessaly.
211 BC	Aetolia allies with Rome.	198 BC	
209 BC	Philip defeats Romans and Aetolians at Lamia.	May	Titus Quinctius Flamininus takes over command of the war against Macedon.
206 BC	Aetolians sign separate peace treaty with Philip; battle of Ilipa occurs.	June	Battle for the Aous gorge; Philip defeated.
205 BC	Rome and Macedon sign the peace of Phoinike to end the First Macedonian War.	September	Battle for Atrax; Flamininus forced to retreat.
203 BC	Philip concludes 'secret' pact with Antiochus III the Great.	September–October	Flamininus marches Roman army into Phocis.
202 BC	Battle of Zama; Philip operates in the Aegean.	October	Achaea joins on the side of Rome.
201 BC	End of the Second Punic War; the battles of Lade and Chios take place; Macedonian attack on Pergamon.	197 BC	
		March	Flamininus captures Thebes and brings Boeotia over to the Roman side.
200 BC	Philip campaigns in Thrace, lays siege to Abydos and rejects Roman ultimatum; start of the Second Macedonian War.	May/June	Cynoscephalae campaign – Philip is decisively defeated.
		December	Peace between Rome and Macedon ratified, end of the Second Macedonian War.
		196 BC	Flamininus proclaims the 'freedom of the Greeks' at the Isthmian Games.

[1] Adapted from Walbank 1940

OPPOSING COMMANDERS

THE ROMAN REPUBLIC

Publius Sulpicius Galba, the Roman consul sent out to Illyria in 200 BC, was a member of one of the most distinguished and ancient patrician *gentes* (clans) of the Roman Republic and early Empire. The Galba branch of the Sulpicii would reach its zenith with the assent of Servius Sulpicius Galba to the imperial purple in 68 AD. Publius Sulpicius Galba was elected consul twice, once in 211 BC and again in 200 BC. In between, he was elected dictator in 203 BC. When elected consul for the first time, he was assigned by lot to deal with Macedonia and as such conducted the military operations against Philip V and Macedon.

He remained in command as pro-consul until 206 BC. Galba played an important role in the lead-up to the Second Macedonian War.

Elected consul in 200 BC for the second time, as well as being assigned, again by luck of the draw, Macedonia as his theatre of operations, Galba convinced the Roman assembly to vote for war with Macedon. Galba appears to have been a competent field commander, but proved ultimately unable in both the First and Second Macedonian Wars to inflict a decisive defeat on Philip V.

Lucius Apustius and **Gaius Claudius Cento** were Galba's senior military deputies. Apustius led a successful raid against Macedon at the start of the campaign, after which he served as a naval commander. He would do so again during the subsequent war against Antiochus III and died leading an assault on the city of Phoenicus. Cento, another Roman legate employed as naval commander, led the successful naval assault on Chalcis in 200 BC.

Publius Villius Tappulus was the elected consul for 199 BC and replaced Galba in command. He arrived late and was unable to achieve much before being replaced himself.

Titus Quinctius Flamininus took over command from Tappulus in 198 BC as the newly elected consul. Born in about 229 BC, he came from a wealthy family with substantial political capital. In 208 BC, Flamininus was a military tribune and later became a quaestor. From 205 until 202 BC, he was commander of the Roman

Portrait identified as Titus Flamininus now in the Delphi museum. Elected consul before the age of 30, Flamininus shot straight to the top of the Roman political establishment. Through the able handling of the campaign against Philip, he succeeded where his predecessors had failed. (Yair Haklai, CC BY-SA 3.0 https://creativecommons.org/licenses/by-sa/3.0, via Wikimedia Commons)

garrison at Tarentum. The next year (201 BC), Flamininus was a member of a commission assigning land to veterans, and the year thereafter he was part of a commission of three organizing the colony of Venusia. Both were senior positions and appear to have provided Flamininus with a network of support and influence that enabled him to stand for the consulship. The senate made sure it smoothed over any objections to Flamininus standing at such an early age (being not yet 30 years old), and he was duly elected as consul for the year 198 BC. He seems to have had no prior military experience or credentials, apart from garrison duty at Tarentum, but was propelled by his own ambition and powerful connections. Speeding towards the scene of the action in Macedonia (having taken his leave of his consular duties back in Rome early), Flamininus was able to take over command from Tappulus before the latter had engaged Philip. After the Macedonian campaign, Flamininus fought a brief war with Sparta (195 BC) and was heavily involved in negotiations with Seleucid Syria prior to Antiochus III landing in Greece. His political reorganization of Greece and the subsequent Roman withdrawal in 194 BC saw Flamininus widely honoured, including through the unprecedented commissioning, most like by himself, of a gold coin bearing his likeness. Back home in Rome, he was awarded a three-day triumph. More sinister and vindictive was his insistence on the old enemy Hannibal Barca being handed over to Rome (by his Bithynian hosts). This led to Hannibal preferring suicide (183 BC) over Roman imprisonment. Flamininus himself died in 174 BC.

A coin portrait of Titus Flamininus. The coin represents a seminal moment in Roman history, as it is the first securely identified coin portrait of a Roman general. Flamininus is clearly acting here in the mould of a Hellenistic king. (ArchaiOptix, CC BY-SA 4.0 https://creativecommons.org/licenses/by-sa/4.0, via Wikimedia Commons)

Throughout the campaign, Flamininus was ably supported by his elder brother **Lucius Quinctius Flamininus**, who served as his naval commander and mainly operated independently. He again served his brother as legate in the war with Sparta. Elected consul himself in 192 BC, he fought successfully against the Ligurians and Celtic Boii. Subsequently as legate, he was involved in the opening stages of the war against Antiochus III. Lucius was a successful commander in his own right with a track record of successful maritime assaults and sieges.

During the conflict, Rome's commanders could rely on the services of two key allies: **Attalus I of Pergamon** and **Amynander of Athamania**. Attalus was the first king of a Hellenised kingdom in Mysia (north-west Asia Minor) centred on the city of Pergamon, and founder of the Attalid royal dynasty. He was an arch-enemy of Philip V, opposing Macedonian ambitions during the first war with Rome, joining on the side of Rhodes to oppose Philip's operations in the Aegean and calling for Roman intervention. As a monarch and general, Attalus I was, on the whole, very successful. He was victorious in battle against Galatians and Seleucids, and was one of the architects of the successful Roman–Rhodian–Pergamene naval campaign against Macedon.

Portrait head of Attalus I, king of Pergamon. Attalus was a sworn enemy of Philip V and had fought against him during the First Macedonian War. His support for Rhodes thwarted Philip's naval ambitions and he actively worked towards involving Rome in a renewed war with Macedon. (Sergey Sosnovskiy from Saint-Petersburg, Russia, CC BY-SA 2.0 https://creativecommons.org/licenses/by-sa/2.0, via Wikimedia Commons)

Amynander was king of Athamania, a tiny but strategically located kingdom in the Pindus mountain range. He appears to have been instrumental to Rome in bringing the Aetolians over to their side and securing the strategic city of Gomphi. During the war with the Seleucids, he took the side of Antiochus III, and fought against Philip V, now an ally of Rome. He died between 189–186 BC, after which kingship in Athamania was abolished.

ANTIGONID MACEDON

Philip V became king of Macedon aged 17, upon the unexpected demise of his uncle Antigonus Doson. As king, he became almost immediately involved in the Social War fought between 220 and 217 BC, during which he displayed great energy and military capability by leading his men in numerous encounters and sieges. Upon the conclusion of the Social War, Philip misjudged Rome's commitment to upholding its interests in Illyria and as a result the king was forced to fight a long, drawn-out war on multiple fronts against a coalition led by Rome, Aetolia and Pergamon. Despite initially suffering reverses, Philip again demonstrated his skill and energy as a commander, acquiring a reputation for quick marching and personal bravery. He was a quick-thinking and extremely capable commander.

His political skill and acumen, however, were not on the same level as his military capabilities. He misjudged Rome's response to his attempted

A coin of Philip V. The king is depicted with a short beard and the characteristic royal diadem. Philip became king aged 17 and, from the start, was involved in one war after another. As a commander, he excelled in forced marches and the kind of smaller scale engagements so characteristic of Greek warfare. (ArchaiOptix, CC BY-SA 4.0 https://creativecommons.org/licenses/by-sa/4.0, via Wikimedia Commons)

intervention in Illyria, a mistake further compounded by his commitment to an alliance with Hannibal Barca. Philip's activities in the Aegean, leading up to the second war with Rome, equally show that the king had not yet grasped the new geo-political reality and the danger of his enemies' appeals and entreaties to the Roman Republic to join the conflict on their side. After Cynoscephalae, Philip collaborated with Rome in the wars against Nabis of Sparta and Antiochus III of Syria. He sought to rebuild and strengthen his kingdom, focusing on increasing revenue, improving the recruitment base for his armies and focusing his expansive ambitions northward. Factional strife, encouraged by Rome, between his sons led the king to order the death of his youngest son Demetrius in 180 BC. Philip himself died in 179 BC.

During the second war with Rome, Philip V relied on a number of subordinates to carry out independent assignments or lead part of his forces. His most trusted commander appears to have been **Athenagoras**, who commanded the mercenaries in the king's employ. Athenagoras opposed the Roman raid in Illyria in 200 BC and led the cavalry during the fighting of 199 BC. He commanded the advance guard during the Aous gorge campaign.

Another general trusted with independent command by Philip was **Philocles**. As governor of Euboea, Philocles was ordered to invade Attica. Later during the war, he secured Argos for Philip and successfully assisted in the defence of Corinth. Later in life, as ambassador to Rome, he became involved in the intrigues surrounding Philip's younger son Demetrius.

At Cynoscephalae, apart from Athenagoras, who was seemingly present at all major encounters of the war, we know the names, but little else, of three other commanders. **Heracleides of Gyrton** commanded the Thessalian cavalry and **Leon** their Macedonian counterparts. **Nicanor**, nicknamed the Elephant, was in charge of the left wing of the Macedonian phalanx. He previously operated in Attica on the king's behalf.

A bust in the Museo Nazionale Romano identified as Philip V. If correct, the king is shown here without beard. In hindsight, Philip's somewhat rash and reckless foreign policies led to the humbling of Macedon on the battlefield and the end of Macedonian control over Greece. (Livioandronico2013, CC BY-SA 4.0 https://creativecommons.org/licenses/by-sa/4.0, via Wikimedia Commons)

OPPOSING FORCES

THE ROMAN REPUBLIC

The force that Publius Sulpicius Galba took across the Adriatic in 200 BC and campaigned with during 199 BC was a standard consular army consisting of two legions and an equivalent number of Italian allies. A Roman legion during this period consisted of between about 4,200 and 5,000 infantry and 300 cavalry. Rome's Italian allies are said to have contributed typically three times more cavalry than that supplied by Rome itself, although this does not appear to have been a hard and fast rule. The army also included elephants, approximately 20 in total. Galba was thus in command of a force of about 18,000 to 20,000 men. Throughout the three campaigning seasons of the Second Macedonian War, this army, the two Roman legions and their Italian equivalents, formed the core of the fighting force available to the two consuls who succeeded Galba in command. The army, however, would be heavily bolstered both by fresh reinforcements from Italy and the contribution of various local allies. Flamininus, for example, upon arrival in the theatre of operations during 198 BC, brought with him reinforcements from Italy to the tune of 3,000 legionaries, 300 Roman cavalry and a further 5,000 infantry and 500 cavalry supplied by Rome's Italian allies. During 197 BC, in preparation for what turned out to be the final campaign, more Roman and Italian troops arrived on the scene. The sources report 6,000 infantry, 300 cavalry and 3,000 allies from Italy's southern Greek cities. Considering all the reinforcements, it seems very likely indeed that the legions would be at full strength, possibly 5,000 men or more. Hammond (1988) has indeed suggested a strength of 22,000 men for the Roman and Italian infantry fighting at Cynoscephalae. Not all reinforcements, of course, would have been used to fill out the legions. Units would have been required for garrison duties, the guarding of supply lines and to support the naval campaign waged by Flamininus' brother, Lucius. The latter indeed had significant forces at his disposal with which he conducted various sieges and assaults during the war. In the immediate lead-up to the battle, 6,000 Aetolian infantry and 400 cavalry joined the army, as well as a further 2,000 Athamanian and 800 Cretan and Apollonian auxiliaries.

The Roman army drawn up to do battle at Cynoscephalae has thus been estimated by various scholars to consist of anywhere between 26,400 to 32,000 plus men. The lower end of the spectrum assigns the legions and Italian equivalents a complement of 18,000, whereas those favouring a higher

A dramatic depiction of an elephant attack at the battle of Zama. After the war, the Romans forbade the Carthaginians from keeping and training elephants for their armed forces. The Romans themselves, however, had got their hands on a number of captured Carthaginian elephants, some of which were used during the campaign against Macedon. (Henri-Paul Motte, public domain, via Wikimedia Commons)

number give the Roman and Italian infantry their full strength of about 22,000 men. Considering the number of reinforcements received, which if all added to Flamininus' army would give it a total theoretical strength of 42,000 infantry and 2,700 (possibly more) cavalry, it seems likely, therefore, the Roman army did number over 30,000 men. Hammond's (1988) estimation that the Roman army at Cynoscephalae consisted of 22,000 Roman and Italian infantry and totalled about 32,400 men appears to be correct.

The Polybian legion

The Roman army that fought the Second Macedonian War was essentially, in terms of its structure, organization, weaponry and recruitment, the same force that defeated Carthage in the Second Punic War. After suffering a number of terrible defeats, it succeeded in decisively defeating the Carthaginians with the crowning victory of the war, at Zama over Hannibal himself, coming as recently as 202 BC. The force transported across the Adriatic in 200 BC carried with it not only many veterans of that conflict but undoubtedly also a sense of self-confidence in its ability to overcome any foe. At the absolute heart of the army, sent to teach the Macedonian king a lesson, was the manipular legion. It was the iron core around which Roman field armies were built. Its recruitment, equipment and organization have been amply studied and set out in detail elsewhere (see *Roman Republican Legionary 298–105 BC* by Fields [2012] or the *Roman Republican Army 200–104 BC* by Sekunda [1996]). It suffices therefore to provide only a brief sketch of the early 2nd century BC Roman legion.

A Montefortino-type helmet. Helmets such as these derive their name from the first example found in the town of Montefortino in Italy. Feathers could be attached to the knob on top. It was the most common helmet worn by the legionaries during the events of Cynoscephalae. (Dorieo, CC BY-SA 4.0 https://creativecommons.org/licenses/by-sa/4.0, via Wikimedia Commons)

Our primary sources for the mid-Republican Roman army are Polybius and Livy. Polybius in particular provides ample information and analysis of the legion in action and its organization. For that reason, we often refer to the Polybian legion when talking about the Roman heavy infantry forces of this period. The legion Polybius discussed and is personally acquainted with consisted of (on paper) 4,200 infantrymen, to which 300 cavalry were attached. The *hastati* (young adults) and *principes* (older men in the prime of their life) were equipped with a helmet, large shield, sword, two throwing spears (*pila*) and some form of body armour. The *triarii* (older veterans) were endowed with a similar panoply, except for the fact that they carried a large thrusting spear instead of the *pila*, which enabled them to fight as hoplites. All also wore a single shin greave on the left leg. *Velites*, on the other hand, carried no armour, reflecting their lower socio-economic status. The most commonly used helmet during this period was the Montefortino helmet. It was made of copper, and decorative feathers could be attached to a central knob. Etrusco-Corinthian helmets were also used. In terms of body armour, the most affluent soldiers wore a mail shirt or perhaps a muscle cuirass. The younger men of the *hastati* with less financial means made do with a square bronze pectoral protecting only the vital areas of the torso. The same type of shield was used by all three types of legionaries. Referred to as a *scutum*, its shape was oval and convex. As his primary weapon, being a swordsman, the legionary carried the fearsome Spanish sword or *gladius Hispaniensis*. Used primarily for stabbing, it seems to have become a part of the legionary panoply during the Punic wars. *Velites* were proper skirmish troops; unarmoured, they carried seven javelins as well as the Spanish sword. The cavalry troopers, the *equites*, represented the richest and aristocratic section of Roman society. It was only they who were able to afford a costly horse. In terms of their equipment, Roman cavalry had adopted the look of 'Greek' cavalry and wore cuirasses (mail or bronze), coupled with an open bronze helmet, round shield and long spear. The Spanish sword was carried by the cavalry as a side arm.

An Etrusco-Corinthian helmet. Helmets such as these were also worn in the Roman army, often by officers, such as the military tribune depicted on the Ahenobarbus altar. These helmets, although harking back to the classic Corinthian type, were worn high on the head. The eyeholes and nasal guard were, by then, purely decorative. (Metropolitan Museum of Art, CC0, via Wikimedia Commons)

When deployed for battle, a legion would arrange itself in three distinct battle lines formed respectively by 1,200 *hastati*, 1,200 *principes* and finally 600 *triarii*. The *velites* fulfilled a skirmishing function in front of the main formation. This deployment in three lines is known as the *triplex acies* formation, the building block of which is the *maniple*, which in Latin refers to a handful. Ten *maniples* of 120 men made up the first two lines with a final reserve line of ten *maniples* consisting of 60 men each bringing up the rear. The *hastati* and *principes* were possibly deployed six deep, the *triarii*, in order to cover the same frontage, lined up three deep. A distinct feature of the *triplex acies* formation is the way in which individual *maniples* were drawn up. Instead of a deployment in three continuous lines, the *maniples* were deployed in what has been called

Legionaries as depicted on the altar of Domitius Ahenobarbus, which is dated to the late 2nd century BC. The soldiers are depicted with Etrusco-Corinthian helmets, mail shirts and the *scutum*. (Shakko, CC BY-SA 4.0 https://creativecommons.org/licenses/by-sa/4.0, via Wikimedia Commons)

a *quincunx* or checkerboard formation. This refers to a battle array in which a gap was left between each *maniple*. These gaps or intervals were covered by the *maniples* of the subsequent line. The *principes* were thus covering the gaps in the battle line of the *hastati*, and the *triarii* did the same for the intervals left between the *maniples* of the *principes*.

Scholarly opinion is still divided as to how exactly the *triplex acies* system operated in a battle scenario. It has been suggested that if the gaps between the *maniples* were maintained, these represented potential weak spots in the line which could be exploited by an intrepid enemy. It has been postulated, therefore, that before closing with an enemy, the Roman line solidified, closing the gaps between the individual *maniples* of the *hastati*. This could be achieved either by extending the frontage of the *maniple* or, if drawn up two centuries deep, moving the rear century sideways and forward to close the gap. In one solid line, the *hastati* would then continue their advance to within *pilum* range, discharge both javelins, draw swords and charge. The alternative view is that the gaps between the *maniples* remained in place during an engagement and that the gaps in the line were covered by the rear lines. It has been argued that gaps between constituent units did not represent a mortal danger to the legionary formation. If an enemy ventured into one of the gaps between the *maniples* of *hastati*, he would be in a very precarious situation with the *principes* of the second Roman line blocking his front and a *maniple* of *hastati* on either side engaging his flanks (the files on the threatened side peeling off to engage the enemy penetration).

A key feature of the Roman military system was the very large recruitment base from which the legions could draw new recruits. It was the duty of every Roman male to serve in the military when required. It has been calculated that during the height of the Second Punic War, Rome was able to potentially raise 25 legions, which represented a force of 110,000 men. The strength of a legion could also be increased to 5,000 men, raising the numbers even further. It has been estimated that in 213 BC 29 per cent of the Roman adult male population was under arms serving in the legions. Recruits were drafted annually based on need and were required to afford their own weaponry. Once recruited, a man underwent rigorous training,

Example of a *gladius* (top) in its scabbard and in the collection of the Archaeological Museum of Naples. Both the heavy infantry of the legions, the cavalry and the *velites* carried the *gladius Hispaniensis*. Their use appalled the Macedonians. (Dorieo, CC BY-SA 4.0 https://creativecommons.org/licenses/by-sa/4.0, via Wikimedia Commons)

OPPOSITE
Side view of a Montefortino helmet in the Museo Etrusco Guarnacci. The majority of the Roman soldiers at Cynoscephalae would most likely have been equipped with such a helmet. (Dorieo, CC BY-SA 4.0 https://creativecommons.org/licenses/by-sa/4.0, via Wikimedia Commons)

which involved learning how to march, handle a sword and be proficient in various athletic exercises such as running and swimming. The Roman army of this period was no professional armed force, however. It was an army of citizen soldiers mustered for the duration of a specific campaign or war. Men could be called upon for service in the army from the age of 17 onwards. The requirement to serve when needed would remain in place until one reached the age of 46. There was, however, a maximum length of service that a Roman citizen was required to fulfil. This was set at 16 years if serving in the legions and ten years when attached to the cavalry. During the Punic wars and afterwards, when Rome's overseas commitments had increased substantially, legionaries spent ever longer periods under arms away from home. Six years of continuous service, when required, seems to have been the norm during the 2nd century BC. Because legionaries were liable for military service for such a long period of time and were serving ever longer periods of continuous deployment, many were highly experienced veteran fighters. Rome's commanders naturally had a preference to enrol them when recruiting for upcoming campaigns. Many veterans also appear to have been keen to enlist again.

Rome's Italian allies

The legions were supported by a levy of Rome's Italian allies, the size of which was established according to need each year by the senate. By the time of the Second Punic and Macedonian War, a standard field army led by a consul would consist of two legions and an equivalent number of infantry provided by the Republic's Italian allies. The latter were also required to raise a cavalry force three times the size of the Roman cavalry component. Two legions together would furnish 600 Roman cavalry. This meant that an additional 1,800 cavalry were required. The Italian infantry and cavalry appear to have been similarly dressed and equipped as their Roman counterparts. It seems likely also that they fought in a similar manner, adopting a *triplex acies* formation. Instead of the *maniple*, however, it was the cohort, consisting of 400 to 600 soldiers, which formed the basic organizational building block. Twenty cohorts in total thus accompanied a force of two Roman legions on campaign. In battle, the legions would line up in the centre with an *ala* (wing), commanded by Roman officers, of ten cohorts on either side.

The Italian cavalry would join their Roman counterparts on the wings. Interestingly, during this period in time, a fifth of the allied cavalry and infantry was selected by the consul to be used for special duty. Designated *extraordinari*, they were tasked with guarding the consular headquarters in camp and safeguarding the army when on the march.

War elephants

The battle of Cynoscephalae would represent the first time that the Romans would use elephants in battle themselves. After the defeat of Carthage in the Second Punic War, one of the requirements of the peace terms was that the Carthaginians were no longer allowed to have elephants. The remaining elephants were to be handed over to Rome. In subsequent years, some of the surviving elephants would see action with the Roman army, and the campaigns of the Second Macedonian War are the first instances of this, as around 20 elephants were part of the army that Galba landed in Illyria after the outbreak of hostilities. The elephant was of the North African forest variety, now extinct, and was smaller than the African savanna and Indian elephant. There is scholarly debate as to whether or not this elephant would have been able to carry a tower on its back to serve as a fighting platform.

ABOVE
A cast of the Domitius Ahenobarbus relief. In the middle, we see two legionaries and, to the right, a Roman cavalryman. The latter wears a mail shirt and a Boeotian helmet. Roman cavalry of this period had re-equipped themselves as Greek cavalry with round shields and spears. (Shakko, CC BY-SA 4.0 https://creativecommons.org/licenses/by-sa/4.0, via Wikimedia Commons)

Greek auxiliaries

During the Second Macedonian War, Rome allied with various Greek and Hellenistic states that contributed contingents of troops to the war effort. As such, armed forces from Aetolia, Athamania, Achaea, Rhodes, Pergamon and Crete made an appearance at various stages. There is not much to go on with regards to the arms, equipment and appearance of the troops

An example of a *thureophoros*. Named after his shield, the *thureos*, soldiers similarly equipped appear to have become the standard Greek infantryman, replacing the traditional hoplite. Armed with a shorter spear, they could engage both in skirmishing and close combat. (DeFly94, public domain, via Wikimedia Commons)

provided by Rome's Greek and Hellenistic allies. It is very likely, however, that the infantry supplied primarily consisted of soldiers termed *thureophoroi*. Named after the use of their characteristic shield termed *thureos*, most Greek states during the 3rd and 2nd centuries BC employed such troops. Armed with a spear, which could be thrown if required, the soldiers thus equipped had a dual-purpose capability and could fulfil a skirmish role as well as engage in hand-to-hand combat. It is also known that after 207 BC at least part of the Achaean army was rearmed and trained in the Macedonian fashion, meaning equipped as sarissa-carrying *phalangites*. Aetolia appears to have had an elite force, the *epilektoi*, possibly numbering 1,000 men, who fought as hoplites in phalanx formation. The Aetolian cavalry were considered an elite force and singled out for praise during the battle of Cynoscephalae. They were renowned for their skirmishing tactics.

There is a bit more information about the Pergamene or Attalid forces involved in the campaign. Though not present for the final battle, Attalid forces made an appearance at various points during the war. Attalid contingents seem primarily to have been made up of mercenaries recruited from various areas, including Crete, Ionia, Illyria, northwestern Asia Minor and Thrace. Most of these forces were probably lightly equipped, possibly again mostly as *thureophoroi* and troops skirmishing with javelins. The Cretans were presumably archers. There is some evidence also for the use of heavy infantry by the Attalid kingdom, possibly even sarissa-bearing guard units in true Macedonian fashion. They may have formed part of a small standing army into which the citizenry of Pergamon and surrounding areas served.

Naval forces

In parallel with the land war, the second conflict with Macedon saw substantial operations conducted at sea. Rome in collaboration with Pergamon and Rhodes pursued an active naval strategy against Macedonian interests. Operating as a combined fleet, the naval forces available to the allies were substantial. At the start of the conflict, the Romans deployed an estimated 50 to 75 warships to Illyrian and Greek waters. They were supported by Rhodian, Pergamene and Athenian vessels. Livy mentions an initial link-up with three Rhodian *quadriremes* and three Athenian vessels without a protecting deck. The Roman ships are described as *triremes* (Liv.31.22). Livy informs us that during the naval campaign of 199 BC, a further 20 Rhodian decked ships joined the fleet, and the Dalmatian Issaei provided 20 *lembi* (Liv.31.45–46). In 198 BC, the Roman fleet consisted of 56 vessels. There is less information on the size of the Pergamene naval contingent operating in Greek waters during the war, but it is known that in 209 BC, during the First Macedonian War, 35 *quadriremes* were deployed. The Attalid fleet appears to have been of a similar size to the Rhodian, consisting of around 40 heavy warships, and it has been estimated that they probably contributed about 20 of that number to the war against Philip.

ANTIGONID MACEDON

The Antigonid Macedonian army as led by Philip V at Cynoscephalae and his son Perseus at Pydna trace their direct heritage to a reconstitution of Macedonian military power after the political instability visited upon Macedon during the wars of the successors. It is during the reigns of Antigonus II Gonatas and in particular that of Antigonus III Doson that we see emerging in the sources the structure of the army which Philip V had at his disposal during his second war with Rome. The army mobilized for the war consisted of four major components: the pike phalanx, peltasts, cavalry and mercenaries plus auxiliaries. Throughout the three seasons of campaigning, the number of troops deployed varied, depending on need and threat level. We need to remember also that throughout the conflict a large proportion of the Macedonian military, particularly mercenaries, were tied up in garrison duties. During the first campaign of the war, Philip concentrated 20,000 infantry and 2,000 cavalry against Galba and, at the battle of the River Aous, the king had with him about 12,000 *phalangites* and 6,000 light troops. Cynoscephalae, the decisive battle of the war, represented a maximum effort on the part of the Macedonian state in terms of the number of soldiers put into the field. Even so, it appears that the Romans substantially outnumbered their Macedonian adversaries.

A painted soldier from the Petsas' tomb in Lefkadia. The soldier wears the *linothorax*, characteristic linen armour, which most likely would have been the standard form of protection worn by most soldiers, both cavalry and infantry, in Philip's army. The tomb is dated to the end of the 4th century BC. (Ancient painters of Macedonia, Greece, public domain, via Wikimedia Commons)

Recruitment and training

The Antigonid army was recruited through the cities of the realm. It was here that citizens were required to step forward in response to a recruitment order from the king. Each household was required to provide one able-bodied man. Recruits were liable for service in the king's army after celebrating their 19th birthday. This could change, however, during a national emergency. For the Cynoscephalae campaign, Philip called up recruits as young as 16. Having been conscripted, Macedonian citizens were then assigned to serve in either the phalanx, peltasts or cavalry. Wealthier recruits were drafted into the elite units. Mobilization was for the duration of a campaign during which the soldiers received irregular pay. Macedonians would start their military training aged 15. This consisted of becoming proficient in the use of bow and javelin. Training would take place in the local gymnasium. Once drafted into the phalanx, the citizen soldier would be instructed in the drill and commands required to successfully fight in phalanx formation.

The pike phalanx

The pike-bearing *phalangite* made up the largest single component of Philip's army. Ever since the days of Philip II and Alexander the Great, pike phalanxes had been at the core of Hellenistic armies. Sources refer to infantry armed in the Macedonian fashion, to highlight the specific equipment and way of fighting that came with serving in the phalanx, most notably of course the lengthy pike called a sarissa. Sarissas could range between 5m and 8m

Artist reconstruction of the serried ranks of the Macedonian phalanx. The success of this fighting formation depended on its ability to present an impregnable wall of spears to the enemy. Drawn up normally 16 men deep, the spears of the first five ranks would project out in front of the formation. (Edmund Ollier, publication date 1882, public domain, via Wikimedia Commons)

in length. It was the extreme length of the pike that gave the Macedonian phalanx its battle-winning capability. The length of the sarissa enabled the *phalangite* to line up in a close-order formation that projected a hedge of spears beyond its front rank. It was probably held underarm and levelled horizontally. Because of its length, the sarissa needed to be held with two hands. It, therefore, became necessary to carry the shield in such a manner that it left the left hand free to hold the sarissa. The use of a shoulder strap and central armband coupled with a hand grip have been suggested as a way in which this could be facilitated. The shield carried by the *phalangite* came in two sizes, the well-known *pelte* at 60–65cm in diameter and larger varieties of about 74cm. It appears that in the Antigonid army the units composing the main phalanx carried the larger variety of shield.

A *phalangite*'s equipment was further complemented by a helmet, some form of body armour, greaves to protect the shins and, as a last resort side arm, a short sword. A soldier's equipment was provided by the Macedonian state, so a certain amount of uniformity in equipment and appearance of the soldiers of the phalanx is to be expected. There is evidence, however, that a wide variety of helmets were used. The *pilos* or later *konos* helmet appears to have seen widespread use, but there is evidence that Thracian/Attic-style helmets were in use by units of the Antigonid phalanx during the early 2nd century BC. Possibly elite units and/or officers wore more elaborate-style helmets, which could have cheek pieces or crests added. In terms of body armour, the front rank, occupying the most exposed position, and officers most likely wore either the *thorax* or *hemi-thorax* (bronze full- or half-armour muscled cuirass), whereas the rest of the phalanx would have worn the well-known linen cuirass called a *linothorax*.

Organization and tactics

The ideal paper strength of a Macedonian phalanx was considered to be 16,384 men. This topline formation could be broken down into various sub-units from a half-phalanx or wing numbering 8,192 men all the way down to the *syntagma* or *speira*, a square pike block of 16 ranks and 16 files. In between, various other organizational sub-units could be found, such as the

Drawing of a now lost artefact found during excavations at Pergamon. It depicts the Macedonian pike phalanx in action (left-hand figures). Note the use of the *pilos* or *konos* helmet and Macedonian-style shields. The scene is believed to depict the battle of Magnesia fought in 190 BC. (Alexander Conze [1831–1914], public domain, via Wikimedia Commons)

chiarchia of 1,024 men or the *phalangargia* of 4,096 soldiers. Clearly, in order to operate a 16,000-strong phalanx formation effectively, a significant amount of internal organization was required. The Antigonid phalanx seems to have been subdivided into two distinct units titled the Chalkaspides (Bronze Shields) and Leukaspides (White Shields), although recently it has been argued that the latter, rather than referring to *phalangites*, denotes troops armed with an oval *thureos* shield covered by white felt.

A phalanx's battlefield success depended upon its ability to present an immovable front of pikes. It was able to do this by deploying in depth, which would give the formation mass and stamina, and by the ability of the phalanx to operate in close order. Depending on the circumstances, the depth of a phalanx could be adjusted. The standard seems to have been the 16-man file, but this could be increased to 32 or reduced to eight men standing one behind the other. The men of the first five ranks would project their weapons in front of the formation forming the hedge of pikes. Ranks six and above angled their pikes upwards, the forests of shafts protruding in the air providing some protection against enemy missile weapons. The effect of an immovable wall of spear points could be further increased by reducing the spacing between the ranks. The phalanx was able to operate in open order, close order and a locked shields formation called *synaspismos* with the spacing between ranks varying from 192cm to 96cm and finally 48cm. The latter formation was primarily defensive. It has been debated in modern scholarship, however, whether the phalanx was able to adopt such a tightly spaced formation. If shields overlapped, there would be no room for the pikes of the first five ranks to protrude forwards. It has recently been suggested, however, that if the pike was held at face height above the shield this would be possible (Du Plessis 2019).

The open order formation, it has been argued, was used by the phalanx to stab and thrust at a similarly armed opponent, relying upon the long reach of their weapons, whereas the intermediate close-order formation was utilized to advance against the enemy with the pikes held underarm and relying on the forward momentum of the advance. The large depth of the formation (normally 16 men deep) was important in keeping the front ranks in place facing the enemy and providing forward momentum, and the forward movement and pressure of all the men behind would naturally propel the formation forward and prevent the front ranks from stepping back. Reconstructions of the phalanx in action have suggested that against non sarissa-bearing opponents (such as the Romans), the lowered pikes would prevent an enemy with shorter-reach weapons from coming to close quarters with the *phalangites*. As such, a stand-off could develop in which an enemy was pinned in place by the serried pikes, unable to close into contact.

A painting belonging to the Macedonian tomb of Lyson and Kallikles and dated to the late 3rd century BC. Depicted is the military equipment belonging to the deceased. One has been identified as a cavalry officer (right helmet), the other (left helmet) as a member of the Chalkaspides (Bronze Shields) regiment. (Ancient painters of Macedonia, Greece, public domain, via Wikimedia Commons)

When the phalanx advanced, its opponent would either have to retreat or try and stand its ground. If no gaps had appeared in the advancing wall of pikes, this would be very difficult to do and risked impalement. If, however, gaps had appeared in the phalanx, either due to the need to navigate difficult terrain, incurring of casualties or simply the individual sub-units of the phalanx becoming disconnected during an advance, an opponent could take advantage and penetrate the densely packed formation. When this happened, the *phalangites* in the effected parts of the line would need to drop their pikes and rely on their swords for defence, placing them at a disadvantage against trained swordsmen such as the Romans.

The peltasts and the Agema

A formation capable of fighting as part of the main phalanx and operating independently were the peltasts. They were normally 5,000 in number and were armed with the smaller variety of bronze shield called the *pelte*, from which they derived their name. The peltasts were deployed by the Antigonids as multi-purpose troops capable of carrying out assaults and special missions. They seem to have worn lighter equipment and no armour when doing so and, in all likelihood, would have been equipped not with the long and cumbersome sarissa but with a shorter spear. In this capacity, the unit seems to be undertaking a similar role to Alexander's famous *hypaspistai* regiment. A total of 2,000 men of the peltasts were designated as the *Agema*, roughly translated as those who lead or vanguard, and formed the king's elite royal guard. The unit seems to have had the nickname 'conquerors'. Dressed in crimson tunics and carrying gilded weapons, these men were all veterans, and similar to the rest of the peltasts, they could be deployed for special action or stand in the main battle line as part of the phalanx.

In the latter scenario, the *Agema* would presumably be re-equipped with pikes and most likely also body armour. At Cynoscephalae, only the royal guard *Agema* was present; the rest of the peltasts appear to have been deployed defending key garrison towns.

Macedonian and Thessalian cavalry

The Macedonian cavalry of Philip V was no longer the shock unit from the days of Alexander and the early successors. Organized into *ilia* of about 100 men, the Macedonian cavalry seems to have had more of a skirmishing role and operated in close conjunction with light infantry forces on the battlefield. It has been suggested that this perceived change in how Macedonian cavalry operated occurred because of the dominance of the pike phalanx, which was able to ward off the shock tactics of earlier days. It is clear from the sources, however, that the Macedonian cavalry continued, on occasion, to employ shock tactics. Philip V can be seen charging in at the head of his cavalry on multiple occasions.

In terms of equipment, at least some of the cavalry by this time carried large round shields. Some of these shields were reinforced with a central spine or *umbo*, which presumably means that the shields were intended to sustain blows received during close-quarters fighting. The primary weapon of cavalrymen bearing such shields would have been the lance or cavalry spear, the length of which is unclear. Round shields lacking reinforcement would have been more suited to longer-distance skirmishing. Livy's description of Macedonian cavalry advancing and retiring having discharged their weapons is indeed indicative of the use of javelins (Liv.31.55.3). Further protection for the cavalry, at least those expected to engage in close-quarters fighting, was provided by a bronze helmet and a linen cuirass. A semi-circular cloak with a decorated border seems to have been standard issue, the colour of the cloak possibly associated with distinct units. The royal guard cavalry was 400 men strong. Its *ilia* were designated as the Sacred Squadrons. It has been suggested that an identifying feature of the guard cavalry was their saffron yellow cloak with purple border.

Ever since the days of Philip II and Alexander, Thessalian horsemen formed a core component of the mounted arm of the Antigonid kingdom. Known for their use of the rhomboid formation, Thessalian cavalry during the Hellenistic period were utilized as shock troops by Pyrrhus of Epirus during his invasion of Italy. Polybius also praised the ability of the Thessalian cavalry to operate in close-order formation (squadron and column) and notes their unsuitability to fight as skirmishers in open order (Polyb.4.8). In Pyrrhus' day, the Thessalians would have been equipped like the Macedonian companion cavalry carrying a lance but no shield, and there is evidence that the Thessalian cavalry continued to do so during the

A gold coin of Nicomedes II of Bithynia. He reigned from 147 to 127 BC. The coin depicts on the observe a Hellenistic-type cavalryman with lance and large round shield with reinforced *spina*. (Public domain, Bibliothèque nationale de France, Coins, Medals and Antiques department, Luynes.2426 [43-36-15])

3rd and 2nd centuries BC and did not adopt the round shield. In terms of appearance, it has been suggested that they may have continued to wear the characteristic broad-brimmed hat and short riding cape attested in artistic representations dating back to the 6th century BC.

Auxiliaries and mercenaries

A description by Plutarch of the Thracians fighting for Perseus at Pydna in all likelihood would hold true as well for the 2,000 Thracians present at Cynoscephalae. As such, they would have been wielding the infamous *rhomphaia*, a weapon ideally suited to slash and thrust, and carried *thureos* shields. Being unarmoured, they were able to operate in challenging terrain. The 2,000 Illyrians present were most likely equipped as *thureophoroi*. An auxiliary unit deployed by Philip V throughout the fighting, but which is not mentioned at Cynoscephalae itself, is the Cretan archers. They were considered elite and carried composite bows, a shield and wore an open-faced bronze helmet. Cretan archers appear to have excelled in close-range archery, collaborating closely with the Macedonian cavalry during the earlier fighting of the war and being singled out for special assault operations. Cretan archers were highly sought-after mercenaries during the Hellenistic period and were also present in Flamininus' army.

Example of a *linothorax* from the Lyson and Kallikles tomb. It has been identified as belonging to a member of the Chalkaspides regiment, probably an officer. (Ancient painters of Macedonia, Greece, public domain, via Wikimedia Commons)

ORDERS OF BATTLE

THE ROMAN REPUBLIC

FLAMININUS' ARMY AT CYNOSCEPHALAE 197 BC (BASED ON HAMMOND 1988)

Legions and Italian allied infantry: 22,000
Roman and Italian cavalry: 2,000 (possibly an underestimation)
Aetolian infantry: 6,000
Aetolian cavalry: 400
Athamanian infantry: 1,200
Cretans: 800
Total: 32,400

ANTIGONID MACEDON

MACEDONIAN ARMY AT CYNOSCEPHALAE 197 BC

Phalanx: 16,000
Agema peltasts: 2,000
Thracians: 2,000
Illyrians: 2,000
Mercenaries: 1,500
Macedonian and Thessalian cavalry: 2,000
Total: 25,500

OPPOSING PLANS

THE ROMAN REPUBLIC

Having landed his troops in Illyria, Sulpicius Galba's options were limited, for the time being. It was now around mid-September, and the campaigning season was already significantly advanced. There were only a limited number of days left before the weather was likely to take a turn for the worse and make further campaigning an impracticability for all intents and purposes (see Morton 2017 for discussion). Sulpicius, therefore, set out in the time left to him to improve the Roman position in Illyria and lay the groundwork for the next campaigning season. His target would be the strategic city of Antipatreia and the forts defending its approach. Capturing the place would greatly facilitate a Roman advance when the campaigning season would open again the following year. Success here might also convince local power players that the Romans meant business and it would be wise to align with them. It was also important to support Athens, the city being under significant pressure because of the activities of Philip's generals in Attica. As a result, it was decided that Lucius Apustius would lead an incursion in strength into the interior of Illyria and his fellow legate, Claudius Cento, would command a squadron of Roman ships sent in support of Athens to Piraeus with the aim of stopping Macedonian raids coming from Chalcis and Acrocorinth (Liv.31.22.4–7).

A graphic representation of an advancing Macedonian phalanx. The wall of spear points, projected forwards by the first five ranks of the formation, facing the legionaries is very apparent in this image. (F. Mitchell, Department of History, United States Military Academy, public domain, via Wikimedia Commons)

ANTIGONID MACEDON

Philip, for his part, had just returned from Thrace. He would have wanted to rest and recuperate his army. Presumably, part of it was also allowed to go home, at least temporarily, after the rigours of the recent campaigning. The king would have known that the campaigning season was by now too far advanced to enable a significant Roman threat to his position in Illyria to develop. Facing a coalition of Rome, Pergamon, Rhodes and Athens, Philip could expect threats coming from multiple directions on different fronts. The recent mauling of the Macedonian navy meant that he would be unable to challenge control of the seas, leaving the shores of his possessions vulnerable to attack. It is likely, therefore, that the king anticipated a largely defensive war in which he would attempt to fight his adversaries to a stalemate. He had successfully done so during the first war with Rome and, prior to that, during the Social War. Philip had shown himself to be a master of small-scale military actions and sieges and would have been confident in his ability, despite the serious situation into which Macedon now found itself, to obtain a favourable peace by blunting the strikes of his enemies and avoiding defeat in battle. Just as in the previous conflict, his advantage was that of the central position, interior lines of communication enabling the Macedonian army to respond to any threats, and, if a favourable opportunity occurred, strike a blow at his enemies. Philip would also have been comforted by the fact that he was still the leader of the Hellenic Security Pact with its members, though not directly involved in the conflict, allied to Macedon. They could potentially be induced to join the fighting on his side.

THE CAMPAIGN

OPENING MOVES

The Roman attack on Chalcis

As ordered, Claudius Cento had taken a small fleet of 20 *triremes* to Piraeus and was quickly able to put a stop to the Macedonian incursions organized from Philip's bases at Chalcis and Acrocorinth, which had terrorized the countryside of Attica (Liv.31.22.4–7). While there, he learned from informants that the key Macedonian base at Chalcis on the island of Euboea was vulnerable to attack. Livy tells us that both the citizens and the garrison deemed themselves safe from attack and were less than vigilant (Liv.31.23.2–12). This seemed to Cento like an opportunity to strike an early and unexpected blow and he led the fleet out, arriving at Chalcis just before daybreak. Without raising the alarm, an assault party was able to scale the walls and dispose of the sentries, either absent or asleep according to Livy. Their next move was to open the city gates and let in their comrades eagerly waiting outside. Pandemonium and widespread slaughter ensued. Fire was set to stockpiled weapons and food stocks, and civilians and soldiers (including the town's military governor) were slaughtered indiscriminately.

View of Chalcis on Euboea. The city was one of the 'fetters' of Greece. Control of the city made it possible to bypass the traditional chokepoint of Thermopylae. (Jebulon, CC0, via Wikimedia Commons)

A fresco from the House of Menander in Pompeii. Of interest is the figure with the conical cap and small round shield. He has been identified as an Antigonid peltast, presumably equipped for when he was not required to stand in the main battle line. (Harlock81, CC BY-SA 4.0 https://creativecommons.org/licenses/by-sa/4.0, via Wikimedia Commons)

After destroying all statues of Philip V they could get their hands on, the Romans loaded up all their loot and sailed away, back to their base at Piraeus, leaving a smouldering Chalcis behind (Liv.31.24–3).

Cento's raid on Chalcis had been a resounding success, but in the cold light of day, as Livy tells us, it may have been somewhat of a missed opportunity. The Roman forces committed were too small to hold Chalcis against a determined Macedonian counter-attack. Had it been possible to commit a larger force, one of the key strongpoints upon which Philip's military plans relied could have been denied to the Macedonian king and could have severely restricted the movement of his forces southward (Liv.31.23.10–12). The lax Macedonian attitude in this episode is doubly surprising, as Chalcis during the First Macedonian War had also been the focus of Roman attack, with Philip setting out almost immediately with his army to relieve the city (Liv.28.7.2–3). In what must have felt to him like a deja vu moment, the king, upon learning of the disaster, set out again in great haste from Demetrias with a hand-picked force of 5,000 light infantry and 300 cavalry, although this time he was unable to save the town. The scene of utter devastation that awaited him at Chalcis must have been a huge blow, not only with respect to the weaponry and supplies lost and casualties incurred, but also with regards the damage done to the prestige of the Macedonian monarchy and its ability to defend its subjects and allies. An immediate response was required, and Philip was determined to do exactly that.

Philip V versus Athens and skirmishes in Illyria

Whatever Philip's plans may have been before the Roman raid on Chalcis, he now decided upon a lightning strike directed against Athens. The assault on his key fortress dictated a firm and immediate response. The city of Athens provided a suitable target in the remaining weeks left of the campaigning season; it was overdue for punishment for declaring war on Macedon (and harbouring the Roman fleet), and if successfully assaulted, would serve as a statement to both Philip's allies and his enemies that the king meant business. Philip subsequently crossed back from Euboea to the mainland and force marched through Boeotian territory towards Athens.

He nearly succeeded in surprising Athens with the speed of his advance. Just as at Chalcis, security had lapsed and it was only thanks to a scout who observed the Macedonian army from one of the watchtowers in Attica and who was able to reach the city before Philip did, that the Athenian defenders were roused in time to man the city's defences (Liv.31.24.4–6). When the Macedonian forces arrived before break of dawn, the humdrum coming from within the city walls showed that the element of surprise had been lost. The king therefore settled down with his army in front of the city to rest up and plan a conventional assault. The Athenians, however, were seemingly

The ruined remains of the Dipylon Gate at Athens. It was here that Philip met the Athenian sortie, fighting a sharp action in which he threw back the enemy. (Mark Landon [photographed in 1992; digitized in 2021], CC BY 4.0 https://creativecommons.org/licenses/by/4.0, via Wikimedia Commons)

confident enough to take the initiative and marched out of the city gates to offer battle. The city's defenders consisted of hired mercenaries and a force supplied by the king of Pergamon. Perhaps the relatively small force that accompanied the king and the close proximity of the city walls, upon which to fall back if needed, had something to do with this rather bold decision (Liv.31.24.8–11).

Livy (31.24.10–11) reports that, 'Philip, seeing this, thought that he had the Athenians in his hands and that he was about to sate his rage with long-desired slaughter ... and urged his soldiers to take him as their example in the fight and to remember that the standards and the battle-line should be where their king was, and put spurs to his horse, inspired by rage and by the hope of glory.'

Spurring his horse, the king, followed by the cavalry and his infantry forces, charged the enemy formation. There are not many details about the ebb and flow of this clash, but it is clear that vicious hand-to-hand combat ensued, although it is equally apparent from Livy that a long-range exchange of missiles also took place. The Macedonian assault and Philip's energetic conduct drove the Athenian and Pergamene forces back on the (Dipylon) gate from which they had sallied. The king appears to have pursued the retreating enemy a bit too vigorously, fighting his way close to or through the enemy gate. The city wall defenders were unable to take aim for fear of hitting their own side in the press of men and horses. With difficulty and seemingly significant casualties, the Athenian force was able to withdraw back inside the city walls, upon which Philip broke off the engagement and retired with his undoubtedly tired force to set up camp.

The Macedonians now set themselves to ravishing the areas outside the city walls, not exempting temples and tombs (Liv.31.24.18). Even the Academy itself was put to the torch (Diod.Sic.XXVIII.7.1). However, Attalid and Roman reinforcements arriving into Athens forced Philip to relocate his camp further away from the city. From thence, the king attempted to surprise the Athenian fortress at Eleusis, but found the place well guarded. In addition, enemy reinforcements were brought via ship from Piraeus. All this

Macedonian or Thessalian cavalryman from the Alexander Sarcophagus and dated to the late 4th century BC. Note the Boeotian helmet and *linothorax* armour; both continued to be worn throughout the Hellenistic period. The Boeotian helmet and its latter derivatives seem particularly associated with cavalrymen. (Photograph taken by User:Marsyas on 06/09/2000, CC BY-SA 3.0 https://creativecommons.org/licenses/by-sa/3.0, via Wikimedia Commons)

made an attack unadvisable and for the moment Philip abandoned his operations against Athens, taking his army to Corinth, having decided to check in with his Achaean allies and determine their zeal for his cause (Liv.31.25.2).

Philip had learned that the Achaean council was in session at Argos to which he at once sped. The Achaeans were debating the recent renewal of hostilities with the Spartan king Nabis. The Macedonian king, who quite naturally sought to ensure Achaean support in his war with Rome, came up with a 'cunning' plan. He offered the council to take on Nabis for them; all the Achaeans needed to do in return was to provide him with a force of soldiers sufficient to act as garrisons for the Macedonian bases at Chalcis, Oreus and Corinth. The council, naturally, saw through this obvious ruse; once in place these garrisons would effectively serve as hostages to ensure Achaean support for the Antigonid cause. Philip's proposal was conveniently dismissed on the grounds that the council could not debate topics outside of those for which the meeting was called together. Disappointed in his attempt to draw Achaea into the conflict with Rome, the king returned to Corinth and from there marched his forces once more into Attica (Liv.31.25.3–11).

While Philip was at Argos, the Athenians had not been given any respite. The king had ordered Philocles, the Macedonian commander on Euboea, to again operate in Attica. With a force of 2,000 Thracians and Macedonians, Philocles made the fortress at Eleusis his target. The capture of this place would give the Macedonians a key strategic base from which to conduct further operations against Athens. It also provided a clear line of communication, back across the Mount Cithaeron pass, with allied Boeotia. Philocles first tried to use a ruse to capture the place, the plan being to tempt the defenders out by exposing his foragers to an attack. Once the garrison was committed to the sally, a hidden force would rush out and strike. Unfortunately for Philocles, the ambush was discovered and thus came to nothing. The Macedonians and Thracians, dispensing with deception, now attacked the citadel head on but were dispersed with heavy loss. This was the situation when Philip, back with his forces from Achaea, joined up with his commander in front of Eleusis (Liv.31.26.2–4). Philip now had at his disposal the 5,000 troops he had brought from Corinth, 300 cavalry and the 2,000 Macedonians and Thracians under Philocles, minus the losses incurred, of course, during the recent fighting. Nonetheless, the forces at the king's disposal were substantial and he had not yet given up on striking a firm blow.

Philip again endeavoured to take Eleusis, but Roman ships, once more shuttling over reinforcements from Piraeus, doomed his attempt. The Roman naval squadron operating out of Piraeus harbour had been very successful thus far, not only in utilizing the harbour as a base for the attack on Chalcis but also in supporting the Athenian defence of Eleusis. Philip clearly recognized this and decided to launch an assault on Piraeus itself. In order to maximize his chances of success, he sent Philocles off at the same time with half the army to threaten Athens and bottle the defenders up inside the city walls. The king will have hoped that his plan would deny the defenders of Piraeus reinforcements. Despite these preparations, however, the attack failed. In typical Philip style, the king abruptly changed plans and quickly marched his forces back to Athens, undoubtedly with the intent to join up with Philocles and conduct another assault on the city. On route, however, he was surprised by a sudden sortie of enemy cavalry and infantry, and fighting took place among and within the now ruined long walls that connected the harbour of Piraeus with the city of Athens. This episode made the king finally give up on his plans to strike a mortal blow at Athens, perhaps realizing that the spirited defence of the city and the apparent strength of its defences made its immediate capture unlikely. So far, all his assaults had failed, and with the end of the campaigning season fast approaching, it was time to withdraw to Macedon and winter his forces there. So, around November time, Philip marched his army back to Macedon, but not before subjecting Attica to another round of pillaging and destruction, singling out places of worship, going as far as to order the destruction of the building stones themselves, leaving nothing but piles of rubble in the wake of his retreating army (Liv.31.26.4–13).

Depiction of a Thracian warrior (right-hand figure) from the Kazanluk tomb. He is equipped with oval shield and *rhomphaia* and is possibly holding a javelin as well. (Public domain, via Wikimedia Commons)

The Macedonian assault on Attica had proved a failure. Intended to avenge the sack of Chalcis and shore up political support for the Antigonid cause, it had achieved none of these things. Although Philip's troops had fought valiantly and driven back the Athenian sallies, all assaults had failed to achieve their objectives. Furthermore, Achaea had politely declined to become involved in the ensuing conflict and, after Philip's failure in Attica, would be less likely to do so in the future. Philip's ravaging of the Athenian countryside had also not won him any friends (Diod.Sic.XXVIII.7.1).

In the meantime, while Philip and Athens were locked in combat, Lucius Apustius had set off on his raid in force of Macedonian-controlled Dassaretis. The three forts protecting the approaches to the strategic city of Antipatreia were successfully assaulted. Negotiations having failed, the city itself was subsequently stormed and completely destroyed, with all men of military age murdered. Fear of a similar fate resulted in Codrion, another strategic and well-fortified place, submitting to the Romans without a struggle. The town

Hellenistic weaponry as displayed on the temple of Athena Nikephoros, now in the Pergamonmuseum in Berlin. Noteworthy are the *konos*-type helmets, linen corselet, sword and *thureos* shield. All this equipment is believed to represent captured Seleucid weaponry after the battle of Magnesia and as such is more or less contemporary with the events under study in this book. (Dosseman, CC BY-SA 4.0 https://creativecommons.org/licenses/by-sa/4.0, via Wikimedia Commons)

was subsequently garrisoned. Apustius' incursion had been an unqualified success and, laden with booty, his forces now journeyed back, after an estimated three weeks of campaigning (Morton 2017), towards their main army encamped west of the River Apsus. While the Roman army was in the process of crossing back over the Apsus, Athenagoras, the Macedonian commander in the area, caught up with the retreating Romans and fell on their rearguard. Apustius, however, was able to form-up his troops and drive off the Macedonians, who suffered significant casualties (Liv.31.27.2–8). In Illyria, then, just as in Attica (under the personal command of the king), Macedonian forces and interests had met with reversal and defeat. Apustius' actions had pushed Roman-controlled territory further east, establishing a firm zone of control protecting southern Illyria and the Roman interests there. Their northern flank was protected by the alliance with the Illyrian Parthini tribe, whose territory also included the important route west through the Genusus valley (Morton 2017).

SULPICIUS' ASSAULT ON WESTERN MACEDONIA

The Roman advance

Roman success in Illyria produced immediate political consequences. Over the winter of 200/199 BC, three key local players now decided to align themselves with the Roman cause and arrived at their camp to offer their alliance and support. These were Pleuratus, chief of the Illyrian Ardiaei tribe, King Amynander of Athamania, and Bato, leader of the Dardanians. These three monarchs would be useful in any further Roman actions planned for the spring of 199 BC. Amynander, in particular, was deemed to be a useful asset as he carried a certain amount of influence among the Aetolian league, which Rome was pretty keen on bringing once more into the anti-Macedonian alliance (Liv.31.28.1–2). Galba now set himself to planning the upcoming campaign, aiming to make full use of the new allies Apustius' success had won. He himself would take the main Roman army into Dassaretis. The Roman fleet under Apustius, aided by the fleets of Pergamon and Rhodes, would wage a naval war against Macedon's coastal possessions (Liv.31.28.3–4).

It seems Galba envisioned a three-pronged assault in the spring of 199 BC with the Roman army driving further east, the Dardanians and Illyrians assaulting Macedon from the north-west and the Aetolians coming up from the south to attack Thessaly. Unfortunately for Galba, the Aetolians stayed neutral for the time being. Livy reports the Aetolian leader Damocritus being bribed by Philip to ensure this (Liv.31.28.6–32). The Macedonian king was also able to block the Dardanians from joining the fray by strategically positioning a strong force, under the nominal command of his young son Perseus, to hold the passes leading from Pelagonia into Lyncus (Liv.31.28.5). With the rest of his army, Philip would position himself for the moment at Heraclea Lyncestis, where he was well supplied, to contest the anticipated Roman assault, although its exact axis of advance could not yet be predicted, since there were various routes the Roman army could take, the most likely one following the Genusus valley and then continuing either north or

The bottom left and middle helmets represent two styles very common during the Hellenistic period. On the left, we have a Phrygian-type helmet whereas the one on the right is of the *pilos* or *konos* variety. The latter may have been standard issue for Macedonian *phalangites*. (MisterPlus65, CC BY-SA 4.0 https://creativecommons.org/licenses/by-sa/4.0, via Wikimedia Commons)

south of Lake Orchid (see Morton 2017 and Hammond 1966). Philip also concentrated the remainder of his navy under the command of Heracleides at Demetrias in anticipation of a renewed Roman naval campaign (Liv.31.33.4). This then was the situation when, with the coming of spring, Galba put his men on the move. As Livy puts it: 'The consul was not preparing, but actually waging war' (Liv.31.33.1).

Galba was looking to initiate a decisive engagement. His command of the Macedonian campaign had not been extended and he would be replaced in due course by the newly elected consul Publius Villius Tappulus. The outgoing consul would, therefore, seek to defeat the Macedonian king in battle before his replacement could arrive, reaping the glory of ending the Macedonian War for himself. In order to do so, he left winter quarters early (likely during April/March, see Morton 2017), and to facilitate a protracted campaign, his troops carried with them significant supplies of grain, untouched at the moment because the needs of the legionaries were being met by supplies of grain confiscated locally. This strategy also had, as Morton (2017) outlines, the intended aim of drawing Philip out in response to the Roman army plundering its way through the territories of Macedon's allies and dependants.

Galba had with him a strengthened consular army of about 18,000 to 20,000 men, including several elephants (Worthington 2023). He had chosen the Genusus valley route and the Romans were able to make good progress, capturing various forts and towns by force or surrender. A new base camp was established near Lyncus (or Lyncestis) on the River Bevus (Liv.31.33.6). Morton (2017) has suggested the area near modern-day Çërravë in the Korçë valley as the most likely place of the Roman campsite.

The Roman consul was unsure, however, of the whereabouts of Philip and the Macedonian army. He had been informed that the king had left winter quarters, but his direction of march was unknown to him. In order to locate the enemy, Galba ordered a detachment of cavalry to find the Macedonians.

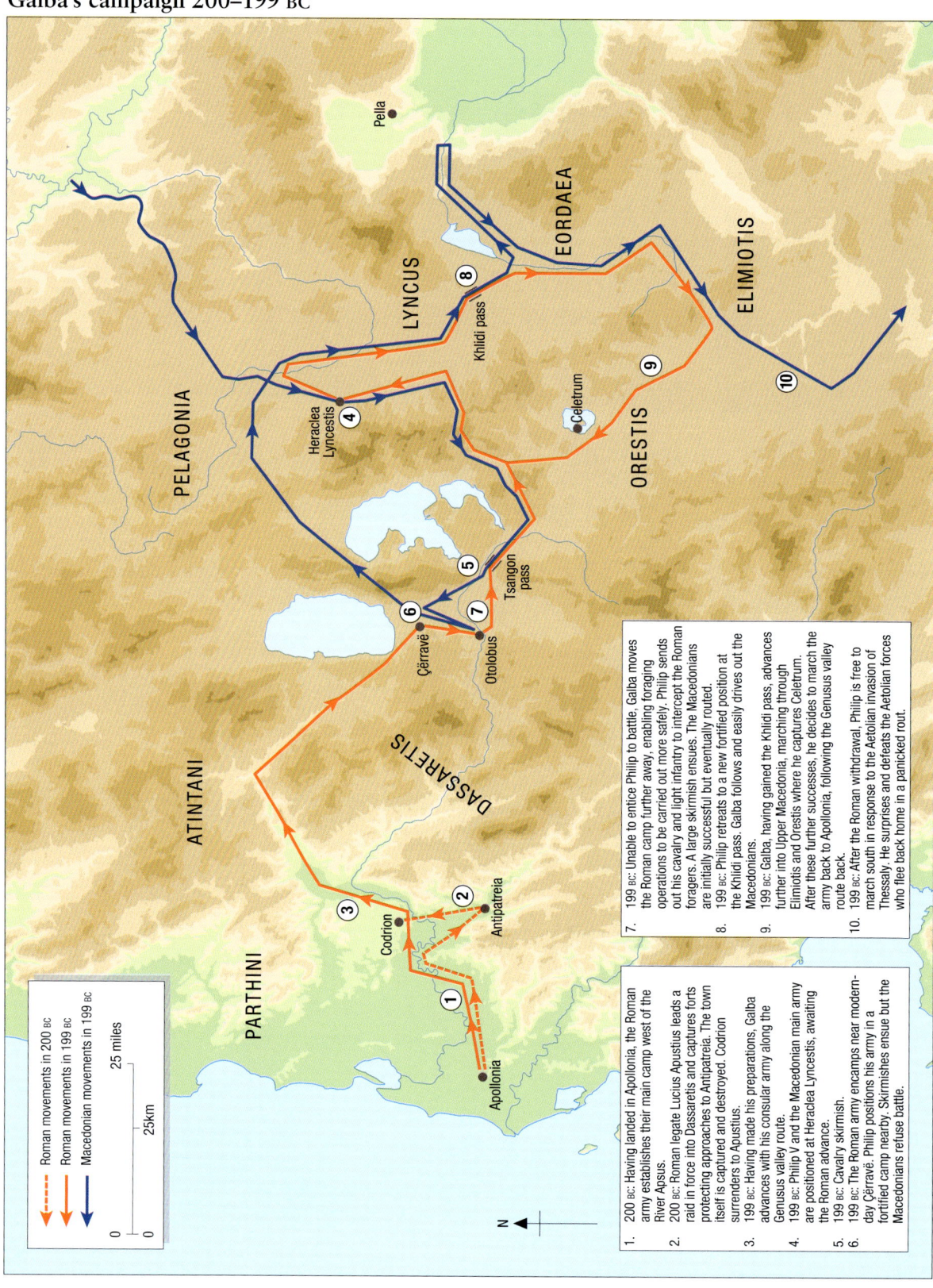

For his part, Philip was equally unsure as to where the Roman army was and had also sent out cavalry tasked to find it. Speeding along the main road through Dassaretis, but from opposite ends, the two forces encountered each other, and a fierce struggle ensued, reported as lasting for several hours. It was only the sheer exhaustion of men and horses that ended the engagement, leaving 40 Macedonians and 35 Romans dead on the field. In the process, neither side had been able to accomplish its mission and actually locate the rest of the enemy army (Liv.31.33.7–11).

This minor skirmish badly affected Macedonian morale. The Macedonians reacted with horror to the wounds their fallen comrades had received. In the words of Livy, 'for men who had seen the wounds dealt by javelins and arrows and occasionally by lances, since they were used to fighting with the Greeks and Illyrians, when they had seen bodies chopped to pieces by the Spanish sword, arms torn away, shoulders and all, or heads separated from bodies, with the necks completely severed, or vitals laid open, and the other fearful wounds, realized in a general panic with what weapons and what men they had to fight' (Liv.31.34.4).

Realizing he would need with him all the soldiers available to combat this formidable adversary, Philip recalled the contingent under his son Perseus guarding the passes to Pelagonia. Reunited, the army under his personal command now consisted of 20,000 infantry and 2,000 cavalry. Deserters had succeeded where the cavalry reconnaissance had failed, and the king was now aware of the location of the Roman army and camp. Marching towards his enemy, Philip selected and fortified a hill not far away from the Roman encampment. From this location, Philip would be able to interfere with and block the Roman advance, offering battle under favourable circumstances and accustoming his main army to its

A depiction of a *thureophoros* from Egypt. He is wearing a crested helmet with ornamental visor and cheek guards. Many of Rome's allies in the conflict with Macedon were probably *thureophoroi*. (Anonymous ancient painter from Ptolemaic Egypt, public domain, via Wikimedia Commons)

The Genusus (currently Shkumbin) river valley. It was this route that Galba and the Roman army took for the campaign of 199 BC. (Römert, CC BY-SA 3.0 https://creativecommons.org/licenses/by-sa/3.0, via Wikimedia Commons)

Two examples of the *gladius Hispaniensis* (Spanish sword). All the Roman combatants carried swords such as these and the damage they were able to inflict caused consternation among the Macedonians, who were unaccustomed to seeing such wounds. (Artistosteles, CC BY-SA 4.0 https://creativecommons.org/licenses/by-sa/4.0, via Wikimedia Commons)

Roman opponents. The king, in the mould of the great Pyrrhus of Epirus, viewing the ordered Roman camp across which he now gazed, is supposed to have commented that 'no one could believe that that camp belonged to barbarians' (Liv.31.44.7).

Confrontation at Çërravë and Otolobus

For Galba, the Macedonian army arriving in strength was undoubtedly the opportunity for which he was looking. The former consul wanted a decisive and potentially war-winning battle to take place before the arrival of his successor. An increasingly dire supply situation, despite the precautions taken, also motivated the Roman general to achieve a quick result (Dio.XVIII.58–1). Philip, however, was less eager to come to conclusions immediately and risk everything on a set-piece battle. Additionally, as Morton (2017) has emphasized, not letting himself be drawn into a set-piece battle was probably the king's strategy all along. Being an experienced campaigner himself, Philip could anticipate the difficulties of supply now besetting the Roman army. Not fighting a battle in this scenario and limiting himself to making life difficult for the Roman foragers offered clear advantages. The Macedonian army therefore remained in its fortified camp on the hill. After two days of waiting for the Macedonians to make a move, Galba decided to lead his army out into the plain between the two camps, taking the initiative by offering battle. The fact that the Macedonians had been sitting inactive in their camp for two days would have enabled Galba to point out to his troops that they feared the Romans, providing an additional morale boost to his army.

The Romans advanced to within a kilometre of the Macedonian camp. In response, Philip ordered his general Athenagoras to take 400 Illyrians, 300 Cretans and 300 cavalry to harass the Roman advance. Galba countered by sending forth his own equally sized force composed of skirmishers and cavalry. The Macedonians were again in for a shock. Macedonian cavalry during this period had more of a skirmishing role fighting with spears and javelins darting in and out of range. The Illyrians and Cretans similarly relied on speed and their ranged weapons to inflict damage upon the enemy. The Romans, in contrast, immediately closed in for hand-to-hand combat after discharging their spears. Lacking sufficient armour and unaccustomed to such close-quarter fighting, Philip's forces were unable to stand up to their opponents, who were well equipped for such fighting with shields and swords, and beat a hasty retreat (Liv.31.35.2–7).

Two days later, Philip sent out Athenagoras again, this time with all of the cavalry (2,000 in number) and the light infantry to skirmish with their opposite number (the main Roman army does not appear to have been drawn up for battle outside the camp this time). The king had also sent out his elite peltasts and deployed them hidden halfway between the two camps. Livy does not provide additional information of the number of peltasts involved, including the elite *Agema*; their number could have been up to 5,000 men strong. If Athenagoras and the cavalry were hard-pressed, they were instructed to retire slowly towards the spot where the peltasts lay in wait, who would then spring up and charge in. Philip was thus hoping to score a morale-boosting victory that hopefully would instil his army with the confidence that it could take on the Romans. Unfortunately for him, the commander of the peltasts sprung the trap too early and the opportunity to surprise their Roman adversaries was lost (Liv.31.36.2–3).

A figure identified as a Macedonian cavalryman on a Roman *denarius* dated to 113/112 BC. The rider is carrying a lance, a round shield with *spina*, and wears a Hellenistic-type crested helmet. (Classical Numismatic Group, Inc. http://www.cngcoins.com, CC BY-SA 2.5 https://creativecommons.org/licenses/by-sa/2.5, via Wikimedia Commons)

The next day, Galba again tried to entice Philip into accepting battle. The Macedonians, however, continued to sit tight on their fortified hill. The Romans, deploying elephants in their line of battle, advanced right up to the Macedonian fortifications, all the time ridiculing their opponents for their cowardice in refusing battle. Philip did not stir. Unable to bring the Macedonians to battle, Galba now decided to move camp. The close proximity to the enemy and the frequent skirmishing posed a danger to his foragers, who were under constant threat from being attacked by the numerous Macedonian cavalry. A new camp was therefore established roughly 12km away at Otolobus. The increased distance between the Roman and Macedonian camps, and presumably also the success of Roman arms up until this point, lured Galba into a false sense of security, and he had no qualms in sending his foragers out to collect grain further away from camp in the surrounding fields. Philip, however, spotted an opportunity and formulated a bold plan. Initially, he did nothing, making the Romans believe he had no intention of interfering with their foraging operations. When, however, the Roman foraging parties were spread far and wide, Philip struck, marching the entirety of his cavalry and his Cretan mercenaries quickly to take up a position between the Roman foragers and their base. Blocking all the roads back to the Roman camp, the king then ordered half his force to attack the foragers and kill as many as it could run down. Great slaughter ensued. The Roman foragers were driven into a frantic flight back to their camp only to run into the Macedonian blocking force. Eventually, some Romans managed to make it back to camp and alert their comrades of the disaster that had befallen them (Liv.31.36.4–6).

Galba reacted immediately upon receiving word of what was happening and sent out his own cavalry in support. Also, mustering his legions, he marched them, drawn up in hollow square formation, towards the fighting. The Roman cavalry appears to have met with little success, seemingly unable to provide effective support to their comrades, who had dispersed far and wide, and were being largely blocked by the Macedonian force under the personal command of Philip straddling the road to the Roman camp. Philip's men, which included the Cretans and royal guard (presumably Livy refers here to the 400-man-strong royal guard cavalry composed of the Sacred Squadrons), were fighting in close-order formation, inflicting many casualties upon the advancing Romans and driving them off. Livy reports that the numbers of men involved at this stage make the encounter 'practically a regular battle'. Having put the Roman cavalry to flight, the king's forces eagerly set off in pursuit, smelling blood. As a result, cohesion was lost and the Macedonian cavalry themselves became disorganized. Right at this moment, the legions arrived on the scene. Taking renewed courage,

PHILIP'S NARROW ESCAPE, JULY 199 BC (PP.46–47)

The Roman cavalrymen, now supported by the upcoming legions, have turned about and routed their Macedonian counterparts, who had become disordered in their overeager pursuit of the fleeing Roman cavalry. Prior to this, the Macedonian cavalry had been very successful in attacking Roman foragers caught out in the open, away from their camp and repulsing the Roman cavalry sent out in support. Philip, in the mould of Alexander, was personally leading the action and his men. Now, however, the tables have turned. Roman cavalrymen are in and among the scattered enemy formation and are striking at the backs of their fleeing foes **(1)**. The Romans are equipped with mail armour, a circular shield, Boeotian or Attic helmets and are fighting with spears and the dreaded Spanish sword (*gladius Hispaniensis*).

Engaged at close quarters by their Roman counterparts, the Macedonians are at a decided disadvantage and the cavalrymen of the royal guard, composed of the Sacred Squadrons, are fleeing the scene of the action **(2)**. They are all wearing saffron yellow cloaks and mostly the *linothorax* for body armour. Macedonian cavalry of this period are seemingly more used to skirmishing, carrying shields for added protection and fighting with javelins. Philip himself is described as fighting with missile weapons from horseback in front of Athens. There is evidence from the sources, however, that elements of the Antigonid cavalry retained a close-combat capability, and Roman and Bithynian coins display Macedonian or Hellenistic cavalry using the large round shield with reinforcing *spina* in combinations with a lance or spear. We have depicted the Sacred Squadrons as such. Helmets worn are varieties of the brimmed *konos* type often depicted in period art.

Cretan archers fighting in tandem with the Macedonian cavalry are caught up in the melee **(3)**. A few are resisting, others are ridden down. Philip himself has been thrown off his horse and is desperately scrambling to his feet **(4)**. The king wears a bronze muscle cuirass and purple cloak and diadem befitting his status as king of the Macedonians. The enemy cavalry is pressing up towards him, keen to capture the Macedonian king. A member of the royal guard cavalry **(5)**, marked out by his saffron yellow cloak, is in the process of dismounting and offering his horse to his king so he can make his escape.

Scene depicted on the Aemilius Paulus monument in Delphi commemorating the Roman victory at the battle of Pydna. To the left, we see a Macedonian cavalryman and a member of the Chalkaspides regiment with characteristic helmet and shield. (Colin Whiting, CC BY-SA 4.0 https://creativecommons.org/licenses/by-sa/4.0, via Wikimedia Commons)

the Roman cavalry turned about and struck back at its over-extended foe. The king's forces were in headlong retreat within moments, pursued by the enemy cavalry and advancing legions. Casualties started to mount and Philip himself was in danger of being overrun by the Romans when he was thrown off his horse. With the enemy cavalry rushing in to intercept him, the king was only saved by the heroic actions of one of his men, who offered Philip his own horse before being struck down by the pursuing enemy. Speeding away, the king and the remainder of his routed forces eventually made their way back to their own camp. Two hundred Macedonian cavalrymen had perished in the battle and a hundred more men were captured as well as 80 horses (Liv.31.37.2–12). Livy does not provide a figure for the number of Romans slain, but considering the nature of the fighting, this was presumably similar.

Again, Philip had been unsuccessful. Although initially victorious, allowing an overeager pursuit had exposed the Macedonians to a determined counter-attack and had resulted in rout and defeat. The king had seen enough. Having been defeated in every clash of arms so far and not wanting to risk further reversals, he decided to withdraw his army. This decision was reinforced by the news that the Dardanians had invaded Macedonia (Liv.31.38.7). The last thing Philip wanted was for his army to become trapped between two enemies. To facilitate breaking off contact with an enemy force in close proximity and get a head start on potential pursuers, the king again resorted to an attempt to trick his opponent, this time successfully. Under the pretext of burying the dead, he sent a herald to Galba suggesting a truce. As soon as darkness fell, however, the Macedonians left their campfires burning and stole away in the dead of night (Liv.31.38.9–10). Finding out in the morning that his opponent had gone and not knowing where to, Galba resigned himself to having lost contact with Philip and focused on the gathering of supplies for his forces (Liv.31.39.2–4).

The Romans next moved on towards Eordaea. Philip, however, had anticipated that this would be Galba's next move and had occupied the pass (Khlidi pass) into Eordaea in order to block the Roman advance. Constructing makeshift fortifications composed of felled trees, ditches and

Funerary relief from Praeneste depicting a large Roman warship dated to the time of the battle of Actium. Throughout the Second Macedonian War, Rome, Pergamon and Rhodes dominated the seas, bottling up the Macedonian navy in port. (Élisée Reclus, public domain, via Wikimedia Commons)

ramparts and using the challenging terrain to their advantage, his men awaited the arrival of the enemy. When arriving on the scene, Galba ordered an immediate attack. Forming *testudo* formation, the legionaries advanced under a hail of projectiles, which did little harm as they were unable to penetrate the Roman shields. The rugged and heavily forested nature of the pass also did not allow the Macedonian and Thracian defenders to wield their sarissas and spears effectively and fight in close order. As a result, the defenders were easily pushed out of the pass and the Roman army gained entry into Eordaea, which was laid to waste. Galba then advanced further into Upper Macedonia marching through Elimiotis and Orestis, where he captured Celetrum (Liv.31.39–40). After these further successes, he decided, however, it was time to turn his army around and march back to Apollonia. The supply situation was again critical, and Galba was unwilling to risk his army further in a country unfamiliar to him and without knowing the whereabouts of Philip and his army (Dio.XVIII.58.1).

The Romans had been extraordinarily successful thus far, besting their opponents on every occasion, although unable to entice Philip into committing himself to a major set-piece battle.

For Philip, the campaign so far had been disappointing. He had been unable to prevent the Roman advance into his territories and dependencies. His strategy of avoiding battle and banking on the Romans running out of supplies had nearly worked, but it seems that the defeat of his forces in every skirmish fought had significantly undermined Macedonian morale and made Philip reconsider his options. A half-hearted attempt to defend the pass into Eordaea had added further insult to injury. The only real bit of good news was that the Dardanian invasion of Macedon had petered out by itself with Athenagoras, the Macedonian cavalry and the light infantry being sent in pursuit to harry the retreating foe (Liv.31.40–43). Ultimately, however, as Philip might have anticipated, the Romans were not able to sustain their campaign and retreated back to their base. Their successful foray into his territories had, however, further undermined Macedon's standing and faith in Philip's ability to defend his allies and interests from the Roman onslaught. Additionally, as Morton (2017) has pointed out, the Romans now controlled the two direct routes from Macedonia into Illyria (via the Genusus valley and Tsangon pass). The situation was further complicated by the operations of Lucius Apustius, Attalus and the Rhodians at sea. While Philip and Galba were engaged on land, sailing from Piraeus, the combined fleet had first captured Andros in the Cyclades before attacking Euboea and taking Carystus and Oreus. The Macedonian fleet, hemmed in at Demetrias throughout the campaign under the command of Hercalides, was unwilling or unable to intervene.

The island of Euboea viewed from the mainland. Carystus and Oreus on Euboea were captured by the Roman, Rhodian and Pergamene naval forces. (George E. Koronaios, CC0, via Wikimedia Commons)

Aetolia joins in

An immediate consequence of Galba's successful campaign of March/April–September 199 BC was the Aetolians joining the war on the Roman side. The Roman victory at Otolobus and the invasion of Macedonia by the Dardanians and Illyrians had convinced the Aetolians they would be backing the winning side (Liv.31.40.9–10). In September, they invaded Thessaly together with King Amynander of Athamania and caused mayhem, attacking and destroying various towns. The Aetolians' success, however, seems to have made them careless and, despite the warnings of Amynander, they made their camp in a spot that was not readily defensible. The king wisely chose to position his men on a nearby hill. He was proved all too right. Philip with his customary energy and speed was advancing against their position, his hands now free after the retreat of both the Romans and Dardanians. The news of his approach caused a panic among the Aetolians, as they were totally unprepared to do battle with the Macedonians. Many were out pillaging or were just waking up from an after-lunch slumber. The men were hastily being drawn up to meet the threat, some unable to get hold of their swords or strap on their armour. They stood no chance and were swept away by the onrushing Macedonian cavalry, fleeing back to camp in disarray. Philip brought up the rest of his army and prepared to attack the Aetolian camp. Before he could do so, however, Aetolian nerves cracked and they rushed out of their camp in headlong flight towards the position of Amynander, suffering many men killed and captured in the process. In the night, the survivors, guided by Amynander, took to the mountain paths in order to escape back to Aetolia, actively pursued the next day by the Macedonian cavalry, which was able to overtake many (Liv.31.41–43). Philip tried to follow up his success by attacking the Aetolian-held Thessalian town of Thaumaci. He employed siege engines and siege works, but it was ultimately in vain, as Aetolian reinforcements were able to cut his lines and reinforce the garrison. The king abandoned the siege at this point and led his undoubtedly weary men back to Macedon to go into winter quarters, bringing the fighting of 199 BC to an end.

The campaign of 198 BC

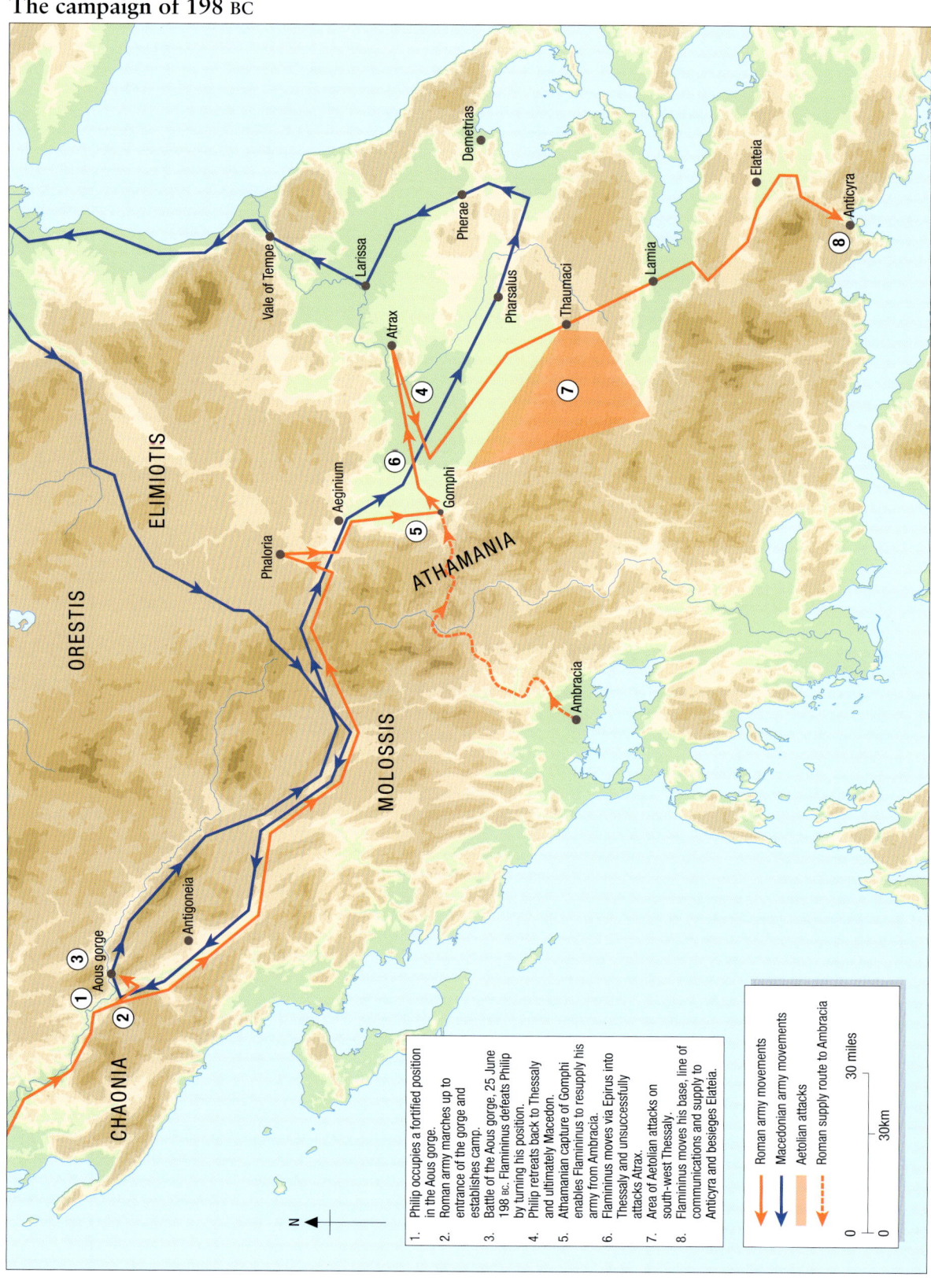

1. Philip occupies a fortified position in the Aous gorge.
2. Roman army marches up to entrance of the gorge and establishes camp.
3. Battle of the Aous gorge, 25 June 198 BC. Flamininus defeats Philip by turning his position.
4. Philip retreats back to Thessaly and ultimately Macedon.
5. Athamanian capture of Gomphi enables Flamininus to resupply his army from Ambracia.
6. Flamininus moves via Epirus into Thessaly and unsuccessfully attacks Atrax.
7. Area of Aetolian attacks on south-west Thessaly.
8. Flamininus moves his base, line of communications and supply to Anticyra and besieges Elateia.

Roman army movements
Macedonian army movements
Aetolian attacks
Roman supply route to Ambracia

The River Aous and gorge. It was here that Philip V and the Macedonian army took up a fortified position. Only an attack in his rear forced the king to abandon his lines. (Thanas Todhe [Guri Q...], CC BY 3.0 https://creativecommons.org/licenses/by/3.0, via Wikimedia Commons)

THE BATTLE FOR THE AOUS GORGE

Philip takes the initiative

Back in Macedon, while giving his men a well-deserved rest, Philip was looking towards the new year with trepidation. His kingdom was now assailed from all sides by its many enemies. Macedon's remaining friends, thus far, had been unable or unwilling to offer much assistance. Livy suggests that Philip at this stage was even doubting the loyalty of his own Macedonians and was worried about his subjects rising up in revolt (Liv.32.5.2–4). The recent successes against the Aetolians and Dardanians could not hide the fact that the war by land and sea was not going well for Macedon. Galba had been able to penetrate Macedonian defences and another Roman invasion of his western territories was in the offing come spring, potentially sowing further seeds of discontent among his subjects and further demonstrating Philip's inability, to his allies, to defend his territories and interests. A different strategy was needed, one that would keep the Roman army as far away from western Macedonia as possible. Philip's experienced eye wandered, therefore, back to Illyria and neighbouring Epirus, and in particular, to the valleys of the rivers Aous and Drin, both of which were accessible to the king and his army via a roundabout route through Epirus, necessary because the Romans and their allies now controlled the most direct routes between Macedon and Epirus. Philip's plan was to take up a strong position on the River Aous. Located here, he would be in a position the Romans would find difficult to ignore without exposing their supply line to a Macedonian attack. The king would also have a safe supply line himself running back through allied Epirus.

With the arrival of spring, Philip put his plan into action. He sent his general Athenagoras into Chaonia (a region of north-western Epirus) with orders to take control of the narrows, the passes leading to Antigoneia. Athenagoras had with him all the light infantry and whatever foreign auxiliaries Philip had been able to muster. The king himself followed a few days later with the main Macedonian field army and, shielded by their compatriots in the narrows, this force was able to take up position in the nearby Aous gorge, which was about 10km in length. The River Aous here flowed through a narrow defile between mountain ranges. Only a narrow road wound

Hellenistic weapons and armour depicted on the balustrade relief of the Athena sanctuary at Pergamon. We see a sword with an eagle hilt, a brimmed *konos* helmet with a decorative visor and a muscle cuirass. Although identified as Seleucid, Philip's troops were most likely similarly equipped. (Carole Raddato from FRANKFURT, Germany, CC BY-SA 2.0 https://creativecommons.org/licenses/by-sa/2.0, via Wikimedia Commons)

itself along the riverbank. Fortifications, consisting of ditches, ramparts and towers, were constructed to further improve the position's natural defences (Liv.32.5.10–13). In places, the cliffs were so steep that they could be defended by only a few men. The battlefield's location and the site of the Roman and Macedonian camps has recently been explored by Morton (2017), who argues for the Macedonian camp to be located in an area of the gorge referred to as the 'Neck'. The river here turns north, and to the east on its southern bank Philip had positioned his main forces. Defensive walls were constructed to defend the riverbank and the camp itself. Significantly, in front of where the heavy infantry was encamped, there was a large open area onto which the phalanx could deploy for action. The king, and his roughly 12,000 *phalangites* and 6,000 light infantry (Morton 2017), now waited for the Romans to respond to this bold stroke.

The Roman army in Illyria had recently said goodbye to its previous commander Galba, who was replaced by the newly arrived consul Publius Villius Tappulus. Upon arrival (in the autumn of 198 BC), Villius almost immediately needed to deal with a mutiny by part of his forces. It was an inauspicious start for the new commander (Liv.32.3.2–7). Things did not proceed much more favourably thereafter. Upon being informed by an Epirote sympathiser of the position the Macedonians had taken up, Villius marched the army up only to find his enemy strongly entrenched. Reconnaissance proved inconclusive as to the best course of action, and the consul spent days debating how to proceed, to force a passage through the enemy or ignore Philip and advance on Macedon itself via the Genusus valley. Unfortunately for Villius, he was never required to make that call as he was to be replaced already. Back in Rome, the elections for the consulship of 198 BC had resulted in Titus Quinctius Flamininus becoming consul and being assigned Macedonia as his province. Plutarch reports that the practice of his predecessors had been to spend a significant amount of their consulship in Rome attending to duties there before setting out towards their allocated provinces and relying on their field commands to be renewed the next year. Flamininus, eager to advance his career, did not want to delay and had sped to the scene of action as fast as he could, thereby depriving Villius of the chance to make a meaningful contribution towards prosecuting the war (Plut.Flam.3.1–2). Come April, therefore, Flamininus was already in Corcyra and soon arrived on the spot to take over command and dismiss Villius (Liv.32.6.2–4).

Flamininus takes command

The new consul, not yet 30 years old, had arrived in the theatre of operations with significant reinforcements. Flamininus brought with him 3,000 Roman infantry and 300 cavalry. The Italian allies of Rome contributed a further 5,000 infantry and 500 cavalry to his force. This was a veteran force composed of soldiers who had previously fought with Scipio in Spain and Africa (Plut.Flam.3.3). With Flamininus came his brother Lucius, who would replace Apustius as the legate in charge of the Roman fleet (Liv.32.8–2). Having dismissed Villius, the new consul found himself in a similar predicament, what to do next? The options available to the commanding general had remained the same and Flamininus, gazing upon the Macedonian position, had a decision to make, to attack frontally or leave Philip where he was and advance on Macedon via Dassaretis. Plutarch indicates that Flamininus was afraid to move his army too far away from the sea (and the provisions that were provided to him by ship). The consul was also worried that doing so would give the Macedonians room to manoeuvre and avoid a decisive battle. He therefore dismissed the option of advancing east through Illyria and the western regions of Macedon. He was going to advance through the gorge and dislodge Philip and his army from the position they had taken up (Plut.Flam.4.1; Liv.32.9–11).

Fragments of a Macedonian shield found at Bonče. It is decorated with a central star and has the typical concentric decoration along its edge. (Beat of the tapan, CC BY-SA 4.0 https://creativecommons.org/licenses/by-sa/4.0, via Wikimedia Commons)

Philip, encouraged by Roman inactivity, decided to use this moment to explore, through the mediation of his ally Epirus, if a negotiated settlement was a possibility. A conference was called with Flamininus and the Macedonian king, who took up positions on either side of the River Aous. The consul's demands were for Philip to withdraw his garrisons from all Greek towns. Thessaly was specifically mentioned as needing to be given up. Philip was outraged. He was willing to restore to freedom the communities he had recently subdued, but categorically refused to hand over those places whose control he had inherited from his forefathers. Unable to find agreement, the conference broke up acrimoniously (Liv.32.10) with the king shouting: 'What heavier condition would you have imposed if you had defeated me in war?' (Diod.Sic.XXVIII.11.1).

He had a point. The Macedonians as of yet were undefeated in a major set-piece battle. There was no way Philip would have been able to agree to Flamininus' demands. Doing so would amount to acquiescing to the dismantling of the Macedonian domination of Greece, for which Philip and his predecessors had fought so hard, and to do so without a proper fight. Clearly, the consul's demands were not designed to find an agreement. Flamininus was in Greece to win laurels. A negotiated peace was not in his interest with the campaigning season having just started and a veteran force at his back.

Battle for the Aous gorge

The next day, skirmishes broke out between the Roman and Macedonian forces. Flamininus had advanced his forces onto the open space in front of the Neck on the river's north bank and they were making good progress, making full use of their discipline and armour protection to force the Macedonians to retreat step by step. When the latter, however, retreated towards the Neck onto more rugged terrain, and under the cover of fire from catapults and *ballistae* positioned on the walls of the gorge, the advance stalled. Casualties now started to mount on both sides, but it was only the advent of nightfall that brought an end to the fighting (Liv.32.10.9-12; Plut.Flam.4.2). Flamininus now realized that a head-on assault on the Macedonian defences was unlikely to pay off. However, the consul may have made multiple attempts over several days to force his way through; the sources are unclear on this. Fortunately for him, a local shepherd was brought into his presence at some point bearing the news that there was a way around the Macedonian position. The man offered to guide the Romans to a location in the rear of the Macedonian army. Having probably no other choice, Flamininus decided to accept this offer, although he kept the poor shepherd in chains throughout. A hand-picked force of 4,000 infantry accompanied by 300 cavalry and led by a tribune was dispatched. Once in position they would send up a smoke signal to alert their compatriots. They marched by night and rested during the day. The cavalry could only follow part of the way, as the ground became too rugged for their mounts to traverse. In order not to alert Philip of the new plan, the consul continued to skirmish with the Macedonian forces for the following two days (Liv.32.11.2–10). It was anticipated the detached force would need three days to get into position, so when the required time had elapsed, Flamininus put in motion his entire force (on 25 June, see Walbank 1940; Morton 2017) and personally led them against the Macedonian defences in the narrowest part of the gorge. At this stage, Flamininus may have already seen the smoke signal or was eagerly scanning the horizon for it.

Pushing the Macedonian skirmishers back, the Romans advanced into the Neck and across the river, which was easily fordable at this point. Overcoming the fortifications protecting the riverfront, the Romans advanced upon the enemy camp. The Macedonians came out to meet them and were able to hold off the Romans. Presumably, Philip had deployed his men in phalanx formation. According to Livy, the Roman force was in danger of being defeated, but it was at just this moment that a smoke signal from the heights dominating the Macedonian position could be clearly seen. A triumphant roar went up among the Roman ranks answered by their comrades coming down the heights and advancing upon the startled Macedonians (Liv.32.12.2-10). The Romans down below also renewed their attack on the Macedonian camp with renewed vigour. Philip's men, caught in the middle and utterly surprised by this attack in their rear, broke almost immediately (Plut.Flam.5.1). With his army routed, Philip sped away from the field, stopping only after about 8km to review his position and make an attempt to rally those of his men that escaped the carnage. Fortunately for him, the nature of the terrain did not allow for effective pursuit, and with many of his soldiers able to get away, his officers were able to round up most of the stragglers. About 2,000 of his men, however, did not make it back (Liv.32.12; Plut.Flam.5.1), having paid the ultimate price.

Battle for the Aous gorge

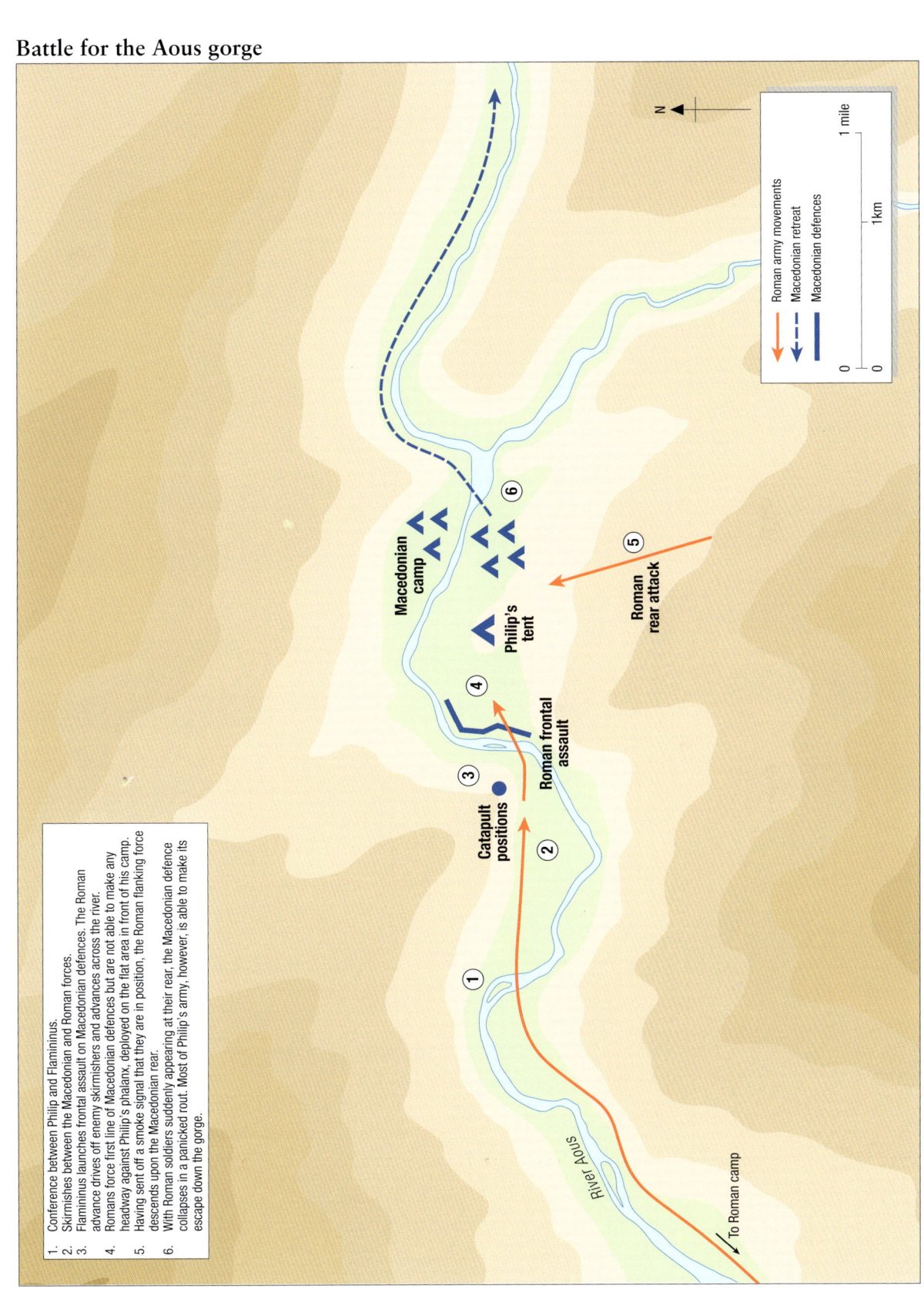

Looking towards the gorge where Philip and the Macedonian army had entrenched themselves from the direction the Roman army would have come up. The Roman camp is about 3km to the north-west. (Calistemon, CC BY-SA 4.0 https://creativecommons.org/licenses/by-sa/4.0, via Wikimedia Commons)

The Romans followed in careful pursuit, hampered by the rough ground and narrow paths. The Macedonian camp was plundered and wounded enemies were dispatched when encountered. After the day's efforts, Flamininus marched his men back to their own camp, where they spent the night (Liv.32.12.7–10). Philip anticipated the Romans to be advancing on Thessaly, and after having considered his position, he decided against retreating to Macedonia itself and instead took his army into Thessaly using the Zygos pass. His aim was similar to before, to deny the advancing Romans easy access to local supplies and resources, the lack of which had previously hampered the advance of Galba. To that end, the king ordered the burning of several towns along his route of march, forcing the unfortunate inhabitants to take with them whatever they could carry (Liv.32.13.2–9). Further Aetolian raids, encouraged by the news of the battle of the Aous gorge, caused more hardship to Thessalian communities (Liv.32.13.10–15). Amynander himself, with the help of a Roman detachment, had succeeded in capturing the strategic town of Gomphi (Liv.32.14.2–3).

Contrary to Philip's expectations, however, Flamininus had not followed the Macedonian army into Thessaly. Instead, the consul had taken his army into Epirus and stayed there. Epirus was nominally an ally of Macedon, but had not been militarily involved in the conflict thus far. Flamininus' excursion into Epirus was designed to detach the Epirote League from the Hellenic Security Pact. Instructing his army to refrain from pillaging and plundering the countryside, Flamininus favourably impressed the Epirotes, with many towns and communities willingly coming over to the Roman side. No doubt the presence of a victorious Roman army marching through their territory would have also impressed upon the local authorities the need to do so. The Roman behaviour also contrasted sharply with the hardship Philip was inflicting upon his own subjects in Thessaly (Liv.32.14.4–6; Plut.Flam.5.2). Furthermore, it would also have been vital for Flamininus, before advancing further, to carefully consider his supply situation and make

A Macedonian coin with the club of Heracles on the observe and on the reverse a helmet. The latter is of the brimmed *konos* variety with cheek guards attached and ornamental visor. (http://cgb.fr/, CC BY-SA 3.0 https://creativecommons.org/licenses/by-sa/3.0, via Wikimedia Commons)

appropriate arrangements to sustain his campaign. The Athamanian capture of Gomphi was key in this respect, as it was only a short distance from Aetolian-controlled Ambracia. Flamininus, therefore, ordered his supply ships into the Ambracian gulf to open up this supply route, sending scouts to ascertain all was ready. So before advancing into Thessaly, the Roman consul had made sure that a major and traditional Macedonian ally had been pacified, leaving his rear and Illyria reasonably secure, and that supplies from the fleet could reach his army. Flamininus had thus created the conditions required for a sustained advance into Thessaly, to which he now set himself and his army (Liv.32.15.5–7).

The Roman breakthrough

It was now August, leaving Flamininus approximately eight weeks to continue his campaign and return his men to winter quarters. It seems clear at this stage that the consul had no intention of going back to Illyria. He intended to break through Macedon's western defences permanently and winter the army much closer to the heart of Philip's power, ideally placed to pick up the fighting again in the next campaigning season – if his command were to be extended that is. In the meantime, there was enough of the season left to weaken the Macedonian position further or defeat the king in battle if he would oppose the Roman advance with his field army.

Flamininus, therefore, advanced the army into Thessaly via the Zygos pass. His first target was the city of Phaloria, which was heavily defended by a garrison of 2,000 Macedonian soldiers. Nonetheless, the consul felt that this place had to be taken. In order to reduce western Thessaly to submission, it was important for the first assault to be successful. Thus, despite a spirited Macedonian defence, the Roman pressure was unrelenting and soon paid off with the city's surrender and subsequent destruction. This had the desired effect, as soon after delegations from two nearby communities visited the Roman camp to offer their submission. Aeginium, however, held out (Liv.32.15.2–4). Plutarch's reconstruction of events is much rosier, indicating that because of their restrained conduct in Epirus, the Romans were welcomed by the Thessalians, who came over to their side (Plut.Flam.5.3). It seems though, reading Livy, that they needed some convincing. The Roman army next marched towards Gomphi, where Flamininus' foresight regarding the supplies required for him to keep campaigning in enemy territory becomes

SKIRMISH AT THE AOUS, 25 JUNE 198 BC (PP.60–61)

It is 25 June 197 BC. Flamininus has just put his entire force into motion and is advancing against the Macedonian positions in the Aous gorge. Banking on the arrival of a detached force towards the rear of the enemy lines, the consul is confident of victory. Preceding the legions are clouds of skirmishers. The *velites* **(1)** surge ahead onto the flat area, which, in the preceding days, has seen repeated skirmishing between the two sides. They are armed with javelins and the Spanish sword. Added protection is provided by a helmet and a round shield. No body armour is worn. Many *velites* **(2)** wear wolfskins over their helmets, possibly a means by which to distinguish themselves from the enemy. In battle, *velites* would normally open proceedings by skirmishing with their opposite number on the enemy side before retiring to the flanks of the formation.

Opposing the Romans are Thracian mercenaries and auxiliaries **(3)**. Thracians were present in Philip's forces throughout his war with the Romans and appear to have been a valued part of his army. Equipped mainly as peltasts with javelins and the *thureos* shield but also the imposing *rhomphaia*, they are slowly retiring from the field **(4)**. Interspersed among their formation are slingers and archers. They wear a variety of coloured tunics and cloaks; only a few are equipped with body armour. Bronze helmets and greaves, however, are a common occurrence, particularly the characteristic Phrygian helmet **(5)**. Thracians could not only be deployed as skirmishers but were also able to engage in close-quarters fighting. Some are indeed standing their ground engaging in hand-to-hand combat with the advancing *velites* **(6)**. The general advance of the legions, with a *maniple* of *hastati* **(7)** sent in support of the Roman skirmishers, necessitates the Thracians, however, to fall back on the defensive positions prepared in front of the Macedonian camp.

The Ambracian gulf. It was here that Flamininus sent his supply ships, enabling him to resupply his army via Gomphi. (ArtaMania, CC BY-SA 4.0 https://creativecommons.org/licenses/by-sa/4.0, via Wikimedia Commons)

apparent. From Gomphi, detachments of troops were marched in relays to Ambracia, where the supply fleet had docked, to gather up the food stocks and bring them back to camp (Liv.32.15.5–7). Running short of supplies after the restrained march through Epirus, the Roman army was fully stocked again and ready to continue the campaign. Thus, despite Philip's scorched earth policy, Flamininus' forward thinking enabled his army to stay in the field and advance upon its next target, the town of Atrax.

The siege of Atrax

Atrax was located 16km from Larissa and was strategically placed upon the River Peneus. It was a key defensive position for Philip and defended by a sizeable garrison of hand-picked men (presumably this means either the best of the *phalangites* or the peltasts). Flamininus did not expect much difficulty, especially as his initial assault was quickly able to destroy a section of the enemy fortifications with a battering ram, enabling his forces access to the town. It was then, however, that difficulties began for the Romans. Instead of panicking and surrendering, the Macedonian garrison drew up in phalanx formation across the gap in the wall, determined to prove the fighting prowess of the Macedonian warrior. The ground in front was strewn with debris from the collapsed wall, hampering any advance, and the flanks of the formation were protected by those parts of the walls still standing. An initial Roman advance failed, enraging Flamininus, and it is worth quoting Livy in full as to what happened next:

> When the Macedonians in close order held before them spears of great length, and when the Romans, hurling their javelins to no purpose, had drawn their swords against this sort of testudo, closely-fashioned as if with shields, they could neither approach near enough to engage hand to hand nor cut off the ends of the spears, and if they did cut off or break any of them, the spearshaft, the broken part being itself sharp, helped, along with the points of the undamaged pikes, to make a sort of wall (Liv.32.17.12–14).

Faced by this immovable wall of spears, the Romans were unable to make any headway and force their way into the town. Seeing no further prospect

The port of Anticyra in Phocis. It was this spot that Flamininus selected as the primary base for his army during the winter of 198/197 BC. The Roman supply fleet would be able to dock here and directly supply the army with its needs. (Geomanjo at Greek Wikipedia, Attribution, via Wikimedia Commons)

of immediately capturing the town and unwilling to commit himself to a siege of long duration, Flamininus withdrew. He was also concerned about the effects of the recent encounter on the morale of his men and did not wish to give the enemy any further opportunities to demonstrate their prowess. Furthermore, the supply situation again required his attention. It was now September, western Thessaly was ravaged by war and Philip's scorched earth policy was hardly suitable to winter his forces (Liv.32.18–23).

Flamininus deemed no harbour on the coasts of Acarnania and Aetolia suitable to accommodate both the Roman supply fleet and provide enough shelter for the army for the duration of winter. He, therefore, cast his eye elsewhere and determined the port of Anticyra in Phocis as ideal for his requirements. There was only one minor inconvenience; Phocis was not yet under his control, it being under the shadow of Macedon. The consul, therefore, moved swiftly, storming or receiving the surrender of various towns in the area, including Anticyra, which gave in after a short siege (Liv.31.18.4–9). His attempt to switch his line of communications and supply had again been an unqualified success. His army was now bedded down on the coast being supplied directly by the fleet, cutting out the arduous journey across the mountains to Gomphi, his previous base of operations. Philip had not interfered at all with his activities. The king had withdrawn with his field army to the Vale of Tempe, shying away from a further major confrontation with Roman arms, and instead focused on sending out detachments of his soldiers to help defend areas under threat (Liv.32.15).

In order to further safeguard his position and establish communications with the Aetolians holding the pass at Thermopylae and at the same time isolating Philip's ally Boeotia, Flamininus attempted to capture Elateia. The town, however, containing a Macedonian garrison, closed its gates to the Roman army and the consul was forced to commence a siege (Liv.32.18.9). While the siege was under way, the Romans received word that in Achaea the leader of the pro-Macedonian faction had been expelled. The new man heading up the council of the league, Aristaenus, was favourably disposed towards Rome and had proposed to join the Roman alliance. This solicited intense debate among the council, which was divided, with some members wishing to honour their long-standing allegiance to Antigonid Macedon and others ready to succumb to the realities of *realpolitik*. Both Macedon and Rome dispatched ambassadors in an attempt to sway the council one way or another. In the end, Philip's proven inabilities to defend his allies and interests (making effective Macedonian military assistance in a conflict with Rome unlikely), and having the Roman army and fleet right on their doorstep, made the difference. The words of Aristaenus, reported by Livy, drive at the heart of the matter:

> Why then does Philip, remaining away, ask our aid, rather than, being present in person, defend us, his ancient allies ... Defend us, do I say? Why did he permit Eretria and Carystus to be captured in that way? Why so many towns of Thessaly? Why Locris and Phocis? Why does he now allow Elateia to be besieged? Why did he leave the passes of Epirus and his impregnable position above the Aous river, abandon the defile which he held and retire far into his own kingdom? It was either under compulsion, or from fear, or by design. If he voluntarily left so many allies to be sacked by the enemy, how can he object if his allies take measures for their own security? If he was afraid, let him excuse also our fear. If he retired because he was beaten in battle, shall we Achaeans, Cleomedon, sustain the Roman attack which you Macedonians did not resist? (Liv.32.19.13–15).

Still the Achaeans were divided and fiercely discussed the matter at hand. In the end, however, they voted to assist the Romans and join the Anti-Macedonian alliance (Dio.58.16).

Attack on Corinth and peace talks

While Flamininus fought against Philip at the battle of the Aous gorge and subsequently campaigned in Thessaly and Phocis, the Roman fleet in conjunction with those of Rhodes and Attalus waged their annual naval campaign against Macedonian interests in the Aegean. Lucius Quinctius Flamininus, older brother of the consul, had been appointed the legate commanding the fleet, taking over command from Lucius Apustius at Piraeus. He conducted successful operations against Macedonian strongpoints on Euboea and succeeded in capturing the harbour of Corinth (Liv.32.16.2–17; Liv.32.17.2–3; Dio.XVIII.58.16). He subsequently attempted, in collaboration with the Achaeans, to capture Macedonian-held Corinth itself, but the attack failed, and the allies were forced to withdraw (Liv.32.23.4–13; Dio.XVIII.58.16).

The events of the previous couple of weeks and the recent fall of Elateia, which had finally succumbed to Flamininus (Liv.32.24.2–7), had shaken Philip. The war was clearly not going in his favour. Apart from the setbacks at Atrax and Corinth, the Roman assault both by land and sea upon his dominion and sphere of influence had been highly successful. What was more, the Roman army was no longer confined to Illyria, separated from the western extremities of Macedon by difficult-to-traverse mountainous country. Instead, Flamininus had been able to break out east and with his base of operations now at Anticyra, the Roman army was ideally placed to commence future operations. Philip decided the time had come to again see if it was possible to reach a negotiated settlement. He was aware of the possibility that Flamininus might be replaced in command by a newly elected consul in the near future. It might, therefore, be in the commander's interest to come to a negotiated settlement, which would enable Flamininus to claim the credit for having ended the war. Philip thus sent out entreaties, and a conference between all the warring parties was agreed upon. The main sticking point was the allies' demand that Philip withdraw from Greece, the debate centring on whether this included the king's recent conquests or also those places he had inherited as king (Liv.32.35.8–12). Upon the insistence of Flamininus, the matter was referred to the senate, with both Philip and his adversaries sending ambassadors to Rome to plead their case.

Modern Thebes in Boeotia. The surprise descent on the city by Flamininus and Attalus removed one of Philip's last remaining allies and opened the way for the final campaign of the war. (Chabe01, CC BY-SA 4.0 https://creativecommons.org/licenses/by-sa/4.0, via Wikimedia Commons)

To allow this to happen a three-month truce was agreed, with Philip required to withdraw his garrisons from both Phocis and Locris (Liv.32.36.8–10). Unfortunately for Philip, his efforts came to naught. The senate confirmed Flamininus in command and gave him full authority to end the war as he saw fit (Liv.32.37.2–6). Flamininus thus presented Philip with two options: to withdraw his garrisons from Greece, including Demetrias, Chalcis and Acrocorinth, or resume hostilities (Liv.32.37.6). When informed of this, the king chose the latter, baulking at giving up the position of dominance in Greece that he and his ancestors had worked so hard to secure. The war would continue.

Final preparations

With a final showdown now seemingly inevitable, both Flamininus and Philip proceeded to prepare as best as they could for the upcoming campaigning season. Having been confirmed in command, the senate had voted the former consul reinforcements to the tune of 6,000 Roman infantry, 300 cavalry and 3,000 allied soldiers. Lucius Flamininus' position as legate commanding the Roman fleet was equally confirmed (Liv.32.28.9–12). In March/April 197 BC, Flamininus marched his army from Elateia to Heraclea and thence to Xyniae on the frontier with Thessaly. Here, 6,000 Aetolian infantry and 400 cavalry joined the army. Flamininus' forces now numbered between 26,000 and 32,000 soldiers, and he felt ready to take the offensive. Philip, in the meantime, assembled all the forces he could muster. He was forced to enlist 16-year-olds and retired veterans to make up for recent losses. The king, with this supreme effort, now commanded 16,000 *phalangites*, 2,000 peltasts, 2,000 Thracians, 2,000 Illyrians, a further 1,500 mercenaries of various nationalities and 2,000 cavalry (Liv.33.4). Concentrating his men at Dion, he set about drilling them extensively to get them ready for the coming storm (Liv.33.3.3–5).

The storm, however, was already breaking. Flamininus had moved to detach Philip's last remaining major ally in central Greece, the Boeotian League, from the Macedonian cause. Doing so would secure also his rear and supply line (Morton 2017). Together with Attalus, he had marched one of his legions into Boeotia and had surprised the city of Thebes, getting a hand-picked force of *hastati* inside before the Thebans had realised what was going on. It subsequently did not prove difficult to convince the League council to side with Rome, the nearby presence of its soldiers ensuring compliance. Flamininus did, however, lose a long-term ally in this endeavour, as Attalus suffered a stroke, from which he would soon die, while addressing the Boeotians (Liv.32.2). With Boeotia now pacified, Flamininus could give Philip his undivided attention.

THE CYNOSCEPHALAE CAMPAIGN

The Macedonian king was still at Dion, getting his forces ready as best as he could for the upcoming campaign. Philip must have realized that the situation was now critical. With the advent of spring, the main strength of the Roman army would be unleashed upon Thessaly, part of which was already beyond his control. How to counter the coming threat? The Macedonian army could be held back behind the protection of the Tempe pass, which blocked the most obvious route into Macedonia. Defending this strong position, however, would mean abandoning Thessaly, something that Philip, as king of Macedon and proud heir to Philip and Alexander, was unable to countenance. Thessaly needed to be defended, but how? Considering the strength of his enemies and recent reverses, it would be unwise and unrealistic to take the offensive, much better as in previous campaigns to utilize the strength of a natural position to try and block the Roman advance. Hopefully, in so doing, he could weather another campaigning season, after which who knew what might happen. Flamininus might be replaced by a new commander and with it the prospect of a negotiated settlement could become a possibility. Failing this, Philip would turn to the vaunted Macedonian phalanx and rely on its prowess to defeat the Roman army in a set-piece battle. Being able to deploy the phalanx on favourable ground was a key consideration with regards to maximizing the likelihood of success in battle and as such was at the back of Philip's mind throughout the campaign.

Having made the decision to defend Thessaly, the king made his preparations. He did not yet know the Roman line of march but could anticipate it being one of two options, either along the Pharsalus–Larissa road or along the coastal road through the Pherae gap further east. These were the two major access points through the Mavrovounion/Karadag range, which separated the south-eastern Thessalian plain from the central plain around Larissa (Hammond 1988). Knowing

The remains of ancient Dion. It was here that Philip assembled and trained his army before moving down towards Larissa. (stg_gr1, CC BY 2.0 https://creativecommons.org/licenses/by/2.0, via Wikimedia Commons)

The Cynoscephalae campaign 197 BC

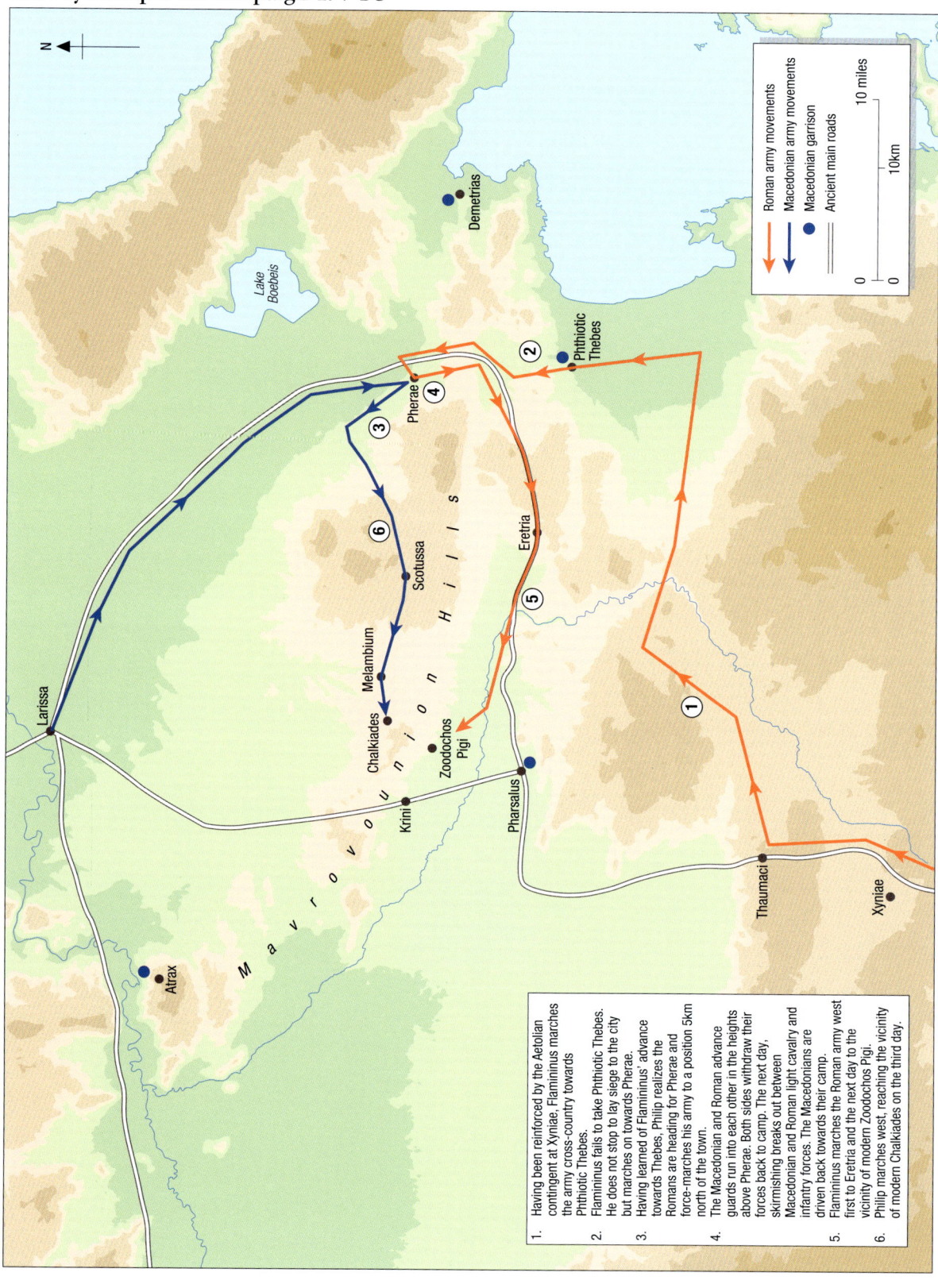

1. Having been reinforced by the Aetolian contingent at Xyniae, Flamininus marches the army cross-country towards Phthiotic Thebes.
2. Flamininus fails to take Phthiotic Thebes. He does not stop to lay siege to the city but marches on towards Pherae.
3. Having learned of Flamininus' advance towards Thebes, Philip realizes the Romans are heading for Pherae and force-marches his army to a position 5km north of the town.
4. The Macedonian and Roman advance guards run into each other in the heights above Pherae. Both sides withdraw their forces back to camp. The next day, skirmishing breaks out between Macedonian and Roman light cavalry and infantry forces. The Macedonians are driven back towards their camp.
5. Flamininus marches the Roman army west first to Eretria and the next day to the vicinity of modern Zoodochos Pigi.
6. Philip marches west, reaching the vicinity of modern Chalkiades on the third day.

that the Romans had wintered at Elateia and in Phocis, Philip anticipated Flamininus would most likely opt to use either of these two principal roads, instead of hooking to the left and advancing on Atrax, where he had previously tasted defeat. Macedonian garrisons in key towns along these access routes would hinder the anticipated Roman advance. Atrax, Pharsalus, Phthiotic Thebes and Demetrias, for example, were garrisoned. The latter was of vital importance for Philip, not only because of its strong garrison but, crucially, for the supplies and provisions it held. If it became necessary to block the Pherae gap with his army, Demetrias would provide a close and secure supply line. The field army, ready to react to whichever move the Romans made, would be held first at Dion and then Larissa, providing the king with a central position from which he could advance in either direction.

Flamininus, having isolated Philip further during March by bringing over Boeotia to the Roman side, now sought a decisive confrontation with the Macedonian army. The war had been going on for the best part of three years and he was determined to end it and reap the political rewards of doing so. The supply situation of the army was also very secure and further improved by the arrival of grain from North Africa, Sicily and Sardinia (Liv.32.27.2). His aim, therefore, would have been to break through Philip's defensive line along the Mavrovounion/Karadag range and force Philip into a decisive battle or to withdraw from Thessaly altogether. Flamininus probably anticipated that Philip would not give up Thessaly completely without a fight. The pro-consul would of course have realized that his adversary was likely to anticipate his advance and move to either block his route by taking up a strong naturally defensive position or offer battle on terrain favouring the deployment of the phalanx. The pro-consul, therefore, seems to have resorted to a ruse. The advance to Xyniae was designed not only to pick up Aetolian reinforcements but, more importantly, also to make Philip think he would drive his army up the Pharsalus–Larissa road. Instead, Flamininus would advance his army cross-country via the Enipeus valley to Phthiotic Thebes, which he hoped to capture by betrayal (Liv.33.5.2–4). From Thebes, it was only a short distance to the gap at Pherae and then into the plain surrounding Philip's primary base at Larissa. A successful advance through the gap would also cut Philip off from Demetrias and isolate its garrison, which might force the king into accepting the hazards of a set-piece battle. Such appears to have been the plan Flamininus conceived and then put into action.[2]

2 See Hammond 1988 for discussion of the chronology of the final campaign of the war. The battle of Cynoscephalae has been placed in May or early June 197 BC by various scholars.

The remains of the ancient theatre in Larissa. Having trained his men, Philip positioned himself at Larissa to await the coming Roman assault. (User:Ggia, CC BY-SA 3.0 https://creativecommons.org/licenses/by-sa/3.0, via Wikimedia Commons)

The advance towards Pherae

Thebes, however, was not betrayed to the Romans. Approaching the town with some cavalry and light infantry, after having marched the entire army on a cross-country route, a sally by its defenders could only be turned back with difficulty and the assistance of reinforcements summoned in support (Liv.33.5.2–3). Undaunted, Flamininus gave up any attempts to capture the town and instead advanced the next day with the army towards Pherae, pitching camp about 50 stades (about 9km) from the town (Polyb.18.19). The next morning, scouting parties were sent out towards Pherae to ascertain the situation and bring news of any enemy movements (Polyb.18.19). While on the march from Xyniae, his army was further reinforced by around 800 archers from Crete and Apollonia. King Amynander also caught up with the army, bringing a further 1,200 infantry. Flamininus' aim most likely would have been to reach the gap before Philip, and as such, no time was to be wasted trying to capture Thebes.

Philip, upon receiving word that the Romans were advancing towards Phthiotic Thebes, realized that Flamininus had stolen a march on him. He reacted swiftly, marching his army off towards Pherae and the gap through the hills. Hurrying his troops along the main road out of Larissa, he was able to establish camp 5.5km outside Pherae. The next morning, the king immediately put his men on the road again, instructing his advance guard to occupy the heights above the town (Polyb.18.19). Possibly, as has been suggested elsewhere (e.g. Hammond 1988), the king was aiming to reach Phthiotic Thebes and give battle to the Romans there. Alternatively, and more likely in the view of the author, Philip wanted to deny the advancing Roman army use of the pass at Pherae.

Contact and break-off

Both the Roman and Macedonian advance guards, therefore, were moving towards Pherae and the gap through the Mavrovounion/Karadag range around about the same time. In the early morning darkness, however, they did not detect each other's presence. It was only when the two converging forces were but a short distance apart that alarm bells started to ring. Having identified the presence of the enemy, both sides halted short of their objectives and sent runners back to their respective commanders asking for instructions (Polyb.18.19). Flamininus and Philip responded similarly and withdrew their advance guard to take stock of the situation. It would have now dawned on Flamininus that he had been unsuccessful in forcing the gap before Philip could arrive. The Macedonian king and his army were in position on the other side of the pass ready to contest occupation of the hilly country around Pherae. What is more, once through the gap, room for manoeuvre would be somewhat restricted with the presence of Lake Boebeis to the east of the Larissa–Pherae road, creating a relatively narrow corridor of flat land upon which Philip could await the Roman advance (the size of the lake varied according to the climate and season; only a corridor roughly encompassing the location of the modern highway provides relatively flat and dry ground, personal communication Prof. Vladimir Stissi).

The next day, skirmishing took place between cavalry and light infantry forces of both sides. There was fierce fighting around Pherae, greatly hindered by the hedges, trees and gardens around the town. The Aetolian cavalry in particular distinguished itself in this engagement and the

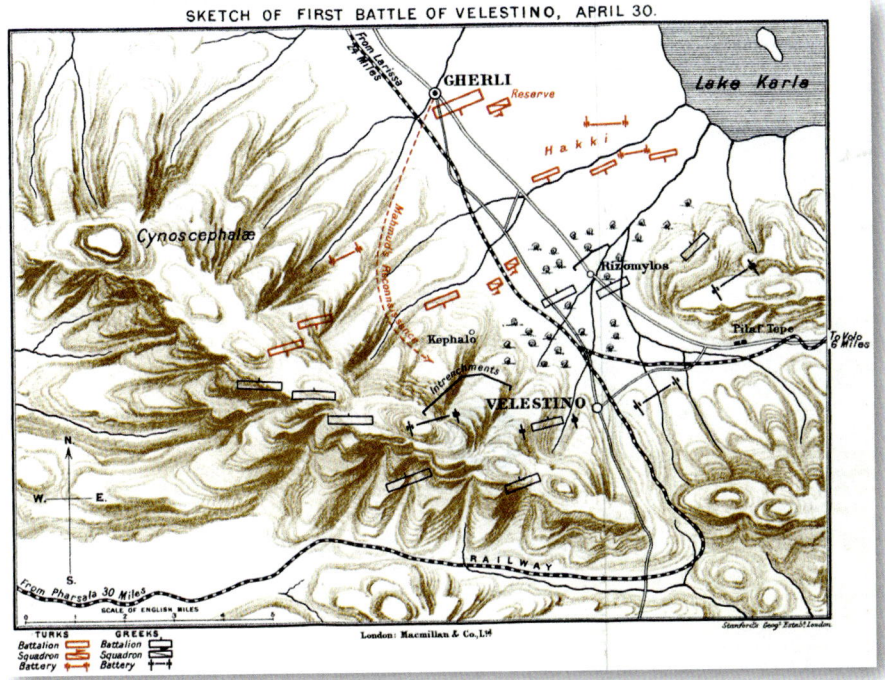

A sketch of Ottoman and Greek positions during the first battle of Velestino in 1897, fought as part of the Greco-Turkish War. Modern Velestino is close to the site of ancient Pherae. Bigham's map allows us to appreciate the way in which the gap through the hills and presence of Lake Boebeis (Karla) would have enabled Philip to take up a strong position. (Charles Clive Bigham; scanned by the British Library; cropped by Constantine, CC0, via Wikimedia Commons)

Macedonians were driven back (Polyb.18.19; Liv.33.6.6–7). The fighting, however, did not materially alter the situation: Flamininus was blocked. His earlier failure to capture Phthiotic Thebes also meant that the Roman army had a hostile garrison at its rear, which could jeopardize supplies coming in from the direction of Xyniae. He also had to contend with the large enemy garrison occupying Demetrias on his right flank. Polybius tells us that both commanders almost simultaneously decided to march their armies off to the west, Philip in search for provisions and Flamininus attempting to prevent this, both marching along parallel lines either side of the Mavrovounion/Karadag range. Polybius also indicates that both commanders were not willing to commit to a major engagement in the broken-up country around Pherae (Polyb.18.20).

It is generally accepted in the literature that Philip moved his army away first. There is debate, however, as to his rationale for doing so. Was it indeed to access provisions in the area of Scotussa where he was now headed or, as has been suggested elsewhere (Livingston and Cole 2015), did the king attempt, by moving away, to lure Flamininus through the Pherae gap, before retracing his steps and cutting the Roman army off from their supply line? Although both Polybius and Livy indicate that Philip moved away first in search of grain, what we know of the strategic situation at the time seems to dictate a different order and motivation to events. Having failed to surprise Philip and with perhaps only a tenuous supply line back towards Pherae, Flamininus could ill afford to remain in position for long. He could try to force his way through the pass, but the terrain around Pherae itself was unsuitable for a set-piece battle, and the main Macedonian army was waiting at the other end of the gap in a strong position. A further advance would also place the Demetrias garrison in his flank and rear, estimated at potentially 5,000 men strong. Philip presumably could have been supplied from Larissa, where his main base was, and thus would probably have been content to

A fountain at the village of Zoodochos Pigi, the name of which means 'life-giving spring'. The presence of a spring here will have made the site a good spot for Flamininus to set up camp. (Photo by Robin Waterfield)

hold his position and let the Romans make the next move. It seems possible, therefore, and perhaps likely, that it was in fact Flamininus who disengaged first and moved west. The bias in favour of Rome on the part of Polybius and Livy may have stood in the way of such a reconstruction of events. A move west in the direction of Pharsalus made sense for Flamininus; it would draw his army not only closer to its supply base but also, with Philip in position at Pherae, provide an opportunity to force his way through the line of the Mavrovounion/Karadag hills elsewhere. If Flamininus did indeed move first, the king naturally would have delayed moving off immediately as well, as he needed to ensure the movement was not a ruse on the part of the Romans designed to draw him away from defending the gap. The pro-consul may have banked, therefore, on getting a head start, which, if all went to plan, would enable him to force his way through the line of hills before Philip could intervene.

Regardless of who moved first, the Roman army marched to Eretria with Philip also moving west, reaching a river called Onchestus by Polybius (Polyb.18.20). Both armies camped at their respective destinations. The next day, while the Macedonian army reached the vicinity of Melambium, identified as being near Agios Konstantinos, Flamininus arrived at a place called the Thetideum, a sanctuary for the goddess Thetis, located in the territory of Pharsalus (Liv.33.6.10–11). The location of this place is disputed. A site that has been proposed and generally accepted as the Thetideum is the modern community of Zoodochos Pigi.

Groping in the mists

The following day, Philip set off early to continue his march. His aim was most likely to reach Paleopharsalus (near modern Krini) and take up position somewhere astride the main road between Pharsalus and Larissa, blocking the anticipated Roman advance. Alternatively, it has been suggested that Philip wanted to connect with his garrison at Pharsalus and/or reach the level plain south of his position and offer battle to the Romans on terrain favourable to his phalanx. Whatever his exact intentions, the king would have been in a hurry to get his men to their destination. To do so he would have to cross the range of hills in between his current position and his intended destination. The weather, however, intervened with a storm, rain and thunder battering the men. Despite setting off, it was much too dark to proceed and visibility was further decreased by a mist rising up from the wet ground (Polyb.18.20). In the words of Livy: 'So dense a fog obscured the day that the standard-bearers could not see the road nor the soldiers the standards, and the column, straggling along in obedience to the various cries, was as disorderly as if wandering about at night' (Liv.33.72).

The king therefore decided to pitch camp, most probably near the modern village of Chalkiades. Recognizing the importance, however, of occupying the strategic high ground, he sent ahead a strong force of infantry and cavalry to take possession of the ridge separating him from his destination (Liv.33.7.3). It is from this range of hills, which separated the two armies moving west, that the now imminent battle would acquire its name. To the ancient observer, the ridge tops looked like dog heads, or *Cynoscephalae* in Greek.

The actual spot where the battle took place is uncertain, and various locations have been proposed (see Hammond 1988 and Butera and Sears 2019). It has been generally accepted, as proposed by Hammond, however, that the battle took place on the range of hills to the north of Zoodochos Pigi. This study, and following recent exploration of the area by Butera and Sears (2019), accepts Hammond's theory and agrees with the identification of the ridge and spurs running between the modern communities of Chalkiades and Zoodochos Pigi as the most likely candidates for the battlefield.

The Romans, in the meantime, seemed to have had a slow start to the day. The heavy rain of the previous evening and early morning, coupled with the dense fog (Liv.33.6.12), had put paid to any plans to march off earlier. Instead, the main army remained in camp and Flamininus restricted himself to sending out 1,000 infantry and ten troops of cavalry to scout ahead and

The ridge line separating the two armies. The initial skirmishes took place on the spur where the houses and trees now are. The part of the phalanx with Philip deployed on this same spur and then charged down the slope to the left. Note the absence of much greenery and the dry and brown colour palette of a Greek summer. (Photo by Matthew Sears and Jake Butera)

THE ADVANCE OF THE MACEDONIAN RIGHT WING, SPRING 197 BC

After the initial skirmishing, which saw the Roman light troops driven down towards their camp, Flamininus deploys his legions, ordering the Roman right wing to hold fast while he takes the left in an uphill advance to support the retreating light troops. Philip V, meanwhile, has just arrived on the ridge with part of his phalanx, which he deploys for action across the Kremaste Spur.

Note: gridlines are shown at intervals of 0.62 miles (1km)

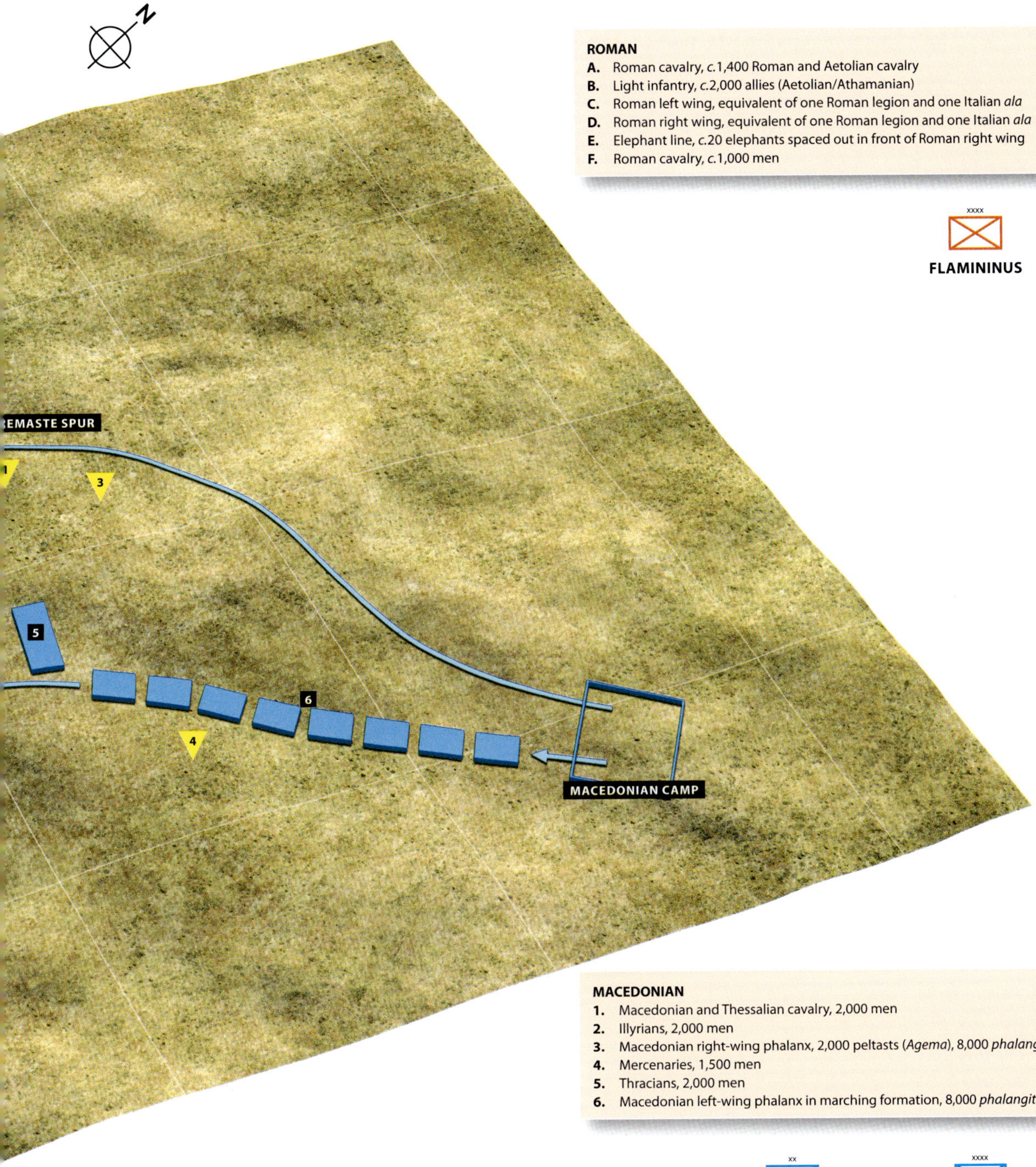

ROMAN
- **A.** Roman cavalry, c.1,400 Roman and Aetolian cavalry
- **B.** Light infantry, c.2,000 allies (Aetolian/Athamanian)
- **C.** Roman left wing, equivalent of one Roman legion and one Italian *ala*
- **D.** Roman right wing, equivalent of one Roman legion and one Italian *ala*
- **E.** Elephant line, c.20 elephants spaced out in front of Roman right wing
- **F.** Roman cavalry, c.1,000 men

FLAMININUS

MACEDONIAN
1. Macedonian and Thessalian cavalry, 2,000 men
2. Illyrians, 2,000 men
3. Macedonian right-wing phalanx, 2,000 peltasts (*Agema*), 8,000 *phalangites*
4. Mercenaries, 1,500 men
5. Thracians, 2,000 men
6. Macedonian left-wing phalanx in marching formation, 8,000 *phalangites*

NICANOR   PHILIP V

EVENTS

1. Philip V sends a strong force of infantry and cavalry to take possession of the ridge separating his army from the plain to the south. A Roman reconnaissance force sent out by Flamininus runs into the Macedonians and fighting ensues.

2. The skirmish on the ridge flows up and down the hillside. Both commanders send reinforcements, with the Macedonians eventually victorious. The Roman light troops are driven down the hill towards their camp. Flamininus brings up the entire Roman left wing in support, leaving his right in reserve.

3. Philip, encouraged by reports from his men, brings up part of the phalanx and deploys them on the Kremaste Spur. Dismayed to find his cavalry and light forces being driven back upon his line by the advancing Roman left, he orders his men to lower their sarissas and advance down the slope.

4. Philip's lieutenant Nicanor, having reassembled the units out foraging, is making his way up the ridge line, aiming to deploy in support of his king.

5. Philip's downhill advance proves unstoppable; the Roman left wing is unable to come to grips with the phalanx and is being driven back steadily down the hill.

discover the whereabouts of his opponents. The pro-consul was wary of marching off with the whole army for fear of running into an ambush, given the prevalent weather conditions. Pressing ahead in the foggy darkness, the Romans quickly and unexpectedly ran into the Macedonian forces, who had taken possession of the hill dominating the ridge.

Initial skirmishes

Having finally regained contact with their foe, both the Macedonians holding the hilltops and the Roman scouting forces rushed off messengers to their respective commanders to apprise them of the situation. Fighting between the forces present then broke out almost immediately as the Romans were advancing up the hill towards the Macedonian position. The king's men were more than holding their own, however; in fact, they were driving their adversaries down the slope. Flamininus, when apprised of the situation, immediately sent off reinforcements, 500 cavalry and 2,000 Aetolian infantry. Reinforced, the Romans and their allies started advancing up the hill again, pushing the Macedonian defenders to the top, where they were trying to make a stand (Liv.33.7.6–8; Polyb.18.21). Philip, back in his camp, now received desperate pleas from his own men for reinforcements. Around the same time, the weather was finally clearing up and the king could see his force crowded together on the hilltop trying to fend off the Romans. Realizing that he risked the utter annihilation of part of his force if he did nothing, Philip turned once more to his trusted commander Athenagoras, sending him off with all the mercenaries (except the Thracians) and the entirety of the Macedonian and Thessalian cavalry. The arrival of this strong force had an immediate impact and, once more, the Romans were driven down the hill and almost back onto the level ground of the valley. It was only due to the heroics of the Aetolian cavalry (considered to be the best in Greece) that an utter rout was prevented (Liv.33.7.9–13; Polyb.18.22).

A view looking north at the spur and ridge as it would have appeared from the Roman camp. The clump of trees in the centre is where the houses of Kremaste are. The fighting between the Macedonian and Roman light forces ranged up and down the spur. Note the landscape, which looks decidedly different in spring as greenery abounds. (Photo by Robin Waterfield)

This second reversal of fortunes prompted Flamininus to lead his legionaries out and draw up his army for battle. Keeping his right wing in reserve, in front of which were drawn up the elephants, he advanced with the left wing, composed of one legion and all the light armed troops, in support of those forces fighting at the base of the hill (Liv.33.8.3–5). Moving among the men, Flamininus spoke words of encouragement, reminding his soldiers of their past successes:

> Are not these the Macedonians, my men, whom, when occupying in their own country the pass to Eordaea, you routed in open battle, under the command of Sulpicius, and drove to take refuge on the hills with the loss of many of their comrades? Are not these the Macedonians whom, when defended by what seemed an impassable country in Epirus, you dislodged by sheer valour, and forced to throw away their shields and fly right into Macedonia? Why then should you feel any hesitation when you are to fight the same men on equal ground? Why look anxiously to the past, rather than let that past minister courage to you for the present? (Polyb.18.23).

While the pro-consul may have spoken words to this effect, Polybius is getting ahead of himself here. Flamininus at this stage would not have known whether the quickly escalating skirmish was going to turn into a full-scale battle. The fact that he left his entire right wing in reserve down in the valley is testament to this. The advance with the left wing was purely designed to support the troops desperately trying to hold their own against the enemy cavalry and light troops. Whether Philip would respond to this further escalation remained to be seen.

Philip brings up the phalanx

On the other side of the ridge, Philip was now receiving glowing reports from his commanders. Elated by their success in driving the Romans down the hill and into the valley, they entreated the king to take advantage of this opportunity and commit the entirety of his army in order to crush the Romans: 'King, the enemy are flying: do not let slip the opportunity. The barbarians cannot stand before us: now is the day for you to strike: now is your opportunity!' (Polyb.18.22).

Philip, being a seasoned commander, was hesitant. First of all, not expecting a battle that day, he had sent off half his men to forage. They were being recalled, but it would take time for the units to form up (Polyb.18.22). Furthermore, the ground on which the engagement was being fought was not ideally suited to deploy his phalanx, being described as rough and steep in our sources. He was also unable to see for himself what was going on exactly on the other side of the ridge. Against his better judgement, however, he was persuaded by the messengers from his commanders on the spot to bring up the main army in support of the troops who appeared to have driven all before them (Polyb.18.22). Having reluctantly made the decision, Philip, without waiting for the entirety of his phalanx to have formed up, took the elite peltasts and his right wing in a rapid advance up the hill. He left instructions for his subordinate commander Nicanor to form up the left wing of the army and follow as soon as possible.

Having ascended the ridge, the scene that greeted him was at first highly pleasing, rousing the king's spirits. His forces were engaged close to the Roman camp and the enemy appeared to be in full retreat.

THE MOMENT OF DECISION, SPRING 197 BC

With the Roman left wing being driven downhill and staring defeat in the face, Flamininus sees the disorderly deployment of the Macedonian left. He transfers himself to the right wing and orders an advance, elephants in the lead, upon the ridge. The Macedonian left wing still in marching order breaks immediately. Twenty detached *maniples* swing into the rear of the Macedonian right and slaughter ensues.

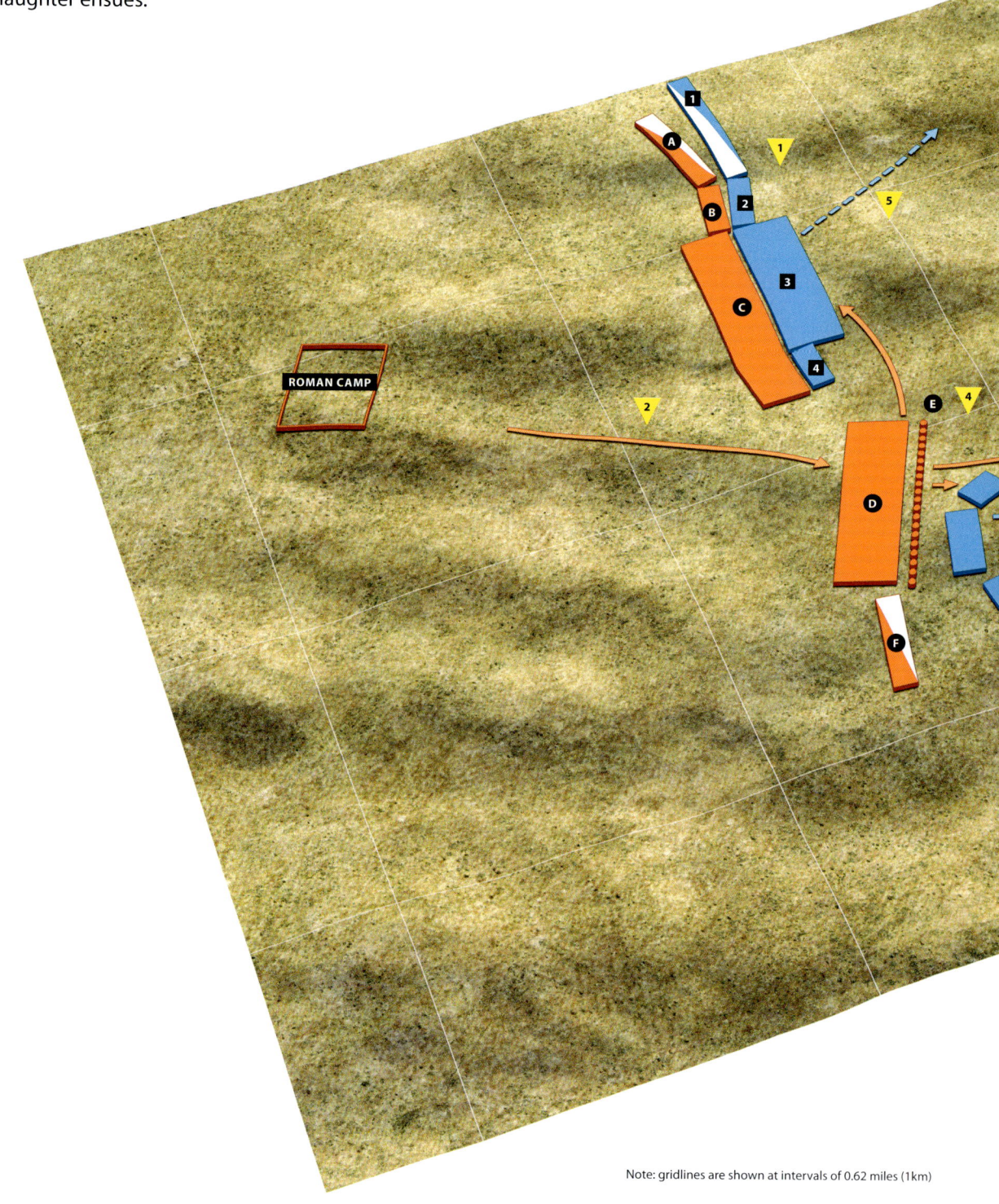

Note: gridlines are shown at intervals of 0.62 miles (1km)

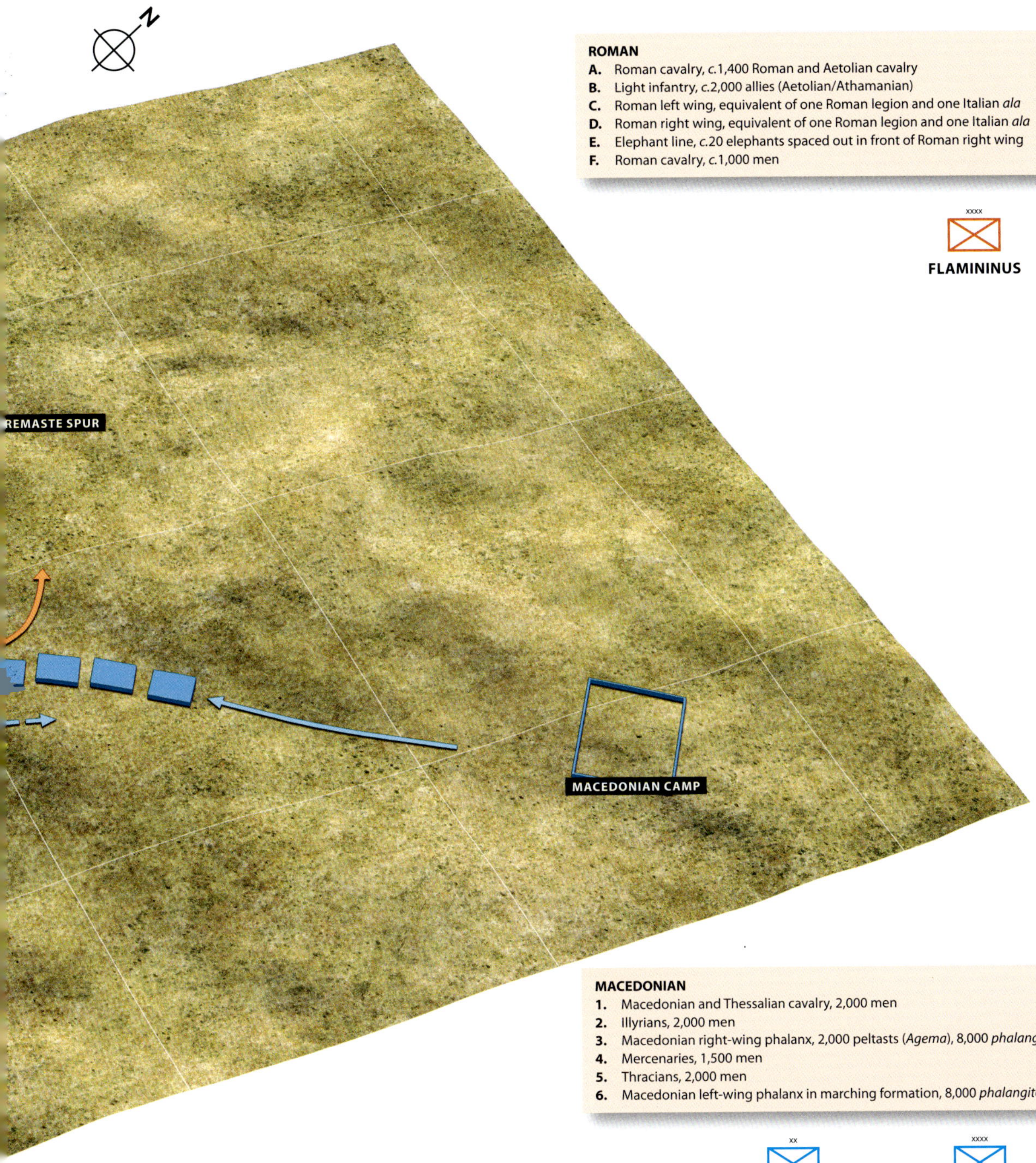

ROMAN
- **A.** Roman cavalry, *c.*1,400 Roman and Aetolian cavalry
- **B.** Light infantry, *c.*2,000 allies (Aetolian/Athamanian)
- **C.** Roman left wing, equivalent of one Roman legion and one Italian *ala*
- **D.** Roman right wing, equivalent of one Roman legion and one Italian *ala*
- **E.** Elephant line, *c.*20 elephants spaced out in front of Roman right wing
- **F.** Roman cavalry, *c.*1,000 men

FLAMININUS

MACEDONIAN CAMP

MACEDONIAN
1. Macedonian and Thessalian cavalry, 2,000 men
2. Illyrians, 2,000 men
3. Macedonian right-wing phalanx, 2,000 peltasts (*Agema*), 8,000 *phalangites*
4. Mercenaries, 1,500 men
5. Thracians, 2,000 men
6. Macedonian left-wing phalanx in marching formation, 8,000 *phalangites*

NICANOR   **PHILIP V**

EVENTS

1. The Macedonian right wing pushes the Roman left ever further down the slope and the legionary formation starts to disintegrate. Victory for Philip on this wing seems imminent.

2. Flamininus, having realized he is in trouble on his left and noticing the Macedonian left-wing phalanx still deployed in marching order atop the ridge, transfers himself to his right and orders an immediate advance towards the enemy left, elephants in the lead.

3. Having failed to properly deploy, the Macedonian left takes one look at the advancing elephants and legion and breaks in rout.

4. While his colleagues are pursuing the fleeing Macedonian left, a tribune detaches 20 *maniples* from the right wing and attacks the Macedonian right in the rear.

5. The Macedonian right, on the verge of victory, is suddenly attacked from behind. Unable to turn and face this new threat, the Macedonians are slaughtered. Philip flees the field.

Philip started to wheel his phalanx into line on the now unoccupied ridge and spur, with the fighting taking place further below. While he was in the process of doing so, the wheel of fortune turned again. Flamininus had led the Roman left wing into action. His light troops, now supported by the heavily armed legionaries, about-faced and pushed back up the slope, causing significant casualties among Philip's men, who retreated, hotly pursued, towards the king's position. Watching aghast at the turn events had taken, the king would have immediately recognized the precariousness of his situation. Below, his forces were in full retreat, with the Romans hot on their heels. Having just arrived on the ridge top himself and with half of the phalanx still marching up the slope, ordering a retreat back to camp would probably end in disaster. With the enemy so close by it would be extremely difficult for the unwieldy phalanx to disengage successfully down a slope. Furthermore, if unsupported, his cavalry and light forces would most probably be completely destroyed. There was, therefore, really only one option left open to the king, to stand firm with his phalanx and prepare to engage the advancing legionaries in open battle (Polyb.18.24; Liv.33.8). Holding the advantage of the high ground and anticipating the speedy arrival of Nicanor and the left wing, a vigorous charge down the slope might prove too much for the enemy to handle. He ordered the phalanx to double its depth and close up ranks (most likely adjusting the formation from eight to 16 ranks deep, although a 32-deep phalanx has also been postulated in the literature). His cavalry and light forces streaming back towards him were redirected towards his right flank (Polyb.18.24).

The attack of the Macedonian right wing

Flamininus responded aggressively to Philip's arrival. Having driven back the enemy light troops and cavalry, he now continued the uphill advance towards that portion of the enemy phalanx that had taken position atop the spur and ridge. While advancing, his *maniples* absorbed their own light

A view from Kremaste looking south in the direction of the Roman camp. This would have been the view of Philip's phalanx as it advanced down the gentle slope rolling back the opposing Roman left wing. The Roman right wing and elephants would have attacked up the spur in the left of the picture. (Photo by Matthew Sears and Jake Butera)

infantry and auxiliaries in the spaces between the units (Polyb.18.24). The Roman right wing remained in reserve on the valley floor. The Roman advance was rapid, and Philip had just enough time to reorganize his forces and get them to form up in line of battle. It seems curious that, considering his experience at Atrax, Flamininus chose to deliver a frontal assault uphill against an enemy force covering roughly equal frontage and cleared for action. Perhaps he hoped to capitalize on the general retreat of Philip's cavalry and light forces, or expected the Macedonian phalanx to be encumbered by the gradient of the slope, offering opportunities for his legionaries to penetrate the enemy formation. Butera and Sears (personal communication) in a forthcoming paper argue that Flamininus had intended all along to fight the Macedonian phalanx on terrain such as that at Cynoscephalae: suitable enough to deploy large numbers of men on but broken up sufficiently to hinder the Macedonian phalanx and favour the more flexible manipular legion. Whatever his considerations, Flamininus was in for a nasty shock. His men were about to bear the full brunt of an advancing Macedonian phalanx.

With the enemy charging towards his line, Philip gave the word and as one the phalanx lowered its sarissas and moved forward (Polyb.18.24). The two sides slammed into each other with great violence; the din of battle was deafening as the war cries of both sides pierced the air. Advancing downhill and with a formation of greater depth and weight, the moving wall of Macedonian spears started to drive back their Roman adversaries. Slowly, the legionaries were required to give ground, unable to stand up to the advancing Macedonians. Looking around, Flamininus saw his casualties mounting as the left wing was given a severe mauling and pushed back (Plut.Flam.8.3). The pro-consul soon realized that the collapse of his left was imminent, and his only hope of averting defeat lay in his as of yet uncommitted right wing. He subsequently hastened himself to his right, leaving his forces on the left to fend for themselves as best as they could.

A view from the Roman camp looking north towards the Kremaste Spur and the ridge where the fighting took place. The Roman left was being driven down the slope of the spur visible in the distance in the centre of the picture. (Photo by Matthew Sears and Jake Butera)

ATTACK OF THE CHALKASPIDES, SPRING 197 BC (PP.82–83)

With the Roman left wing advancing towards his position and his light infantry and cavalry in full retreat, Philip saw no other solution than to prepare the elements of the phalanx with him on the ridge and spur to prepare to receive the enemy. As one, the *phalangites* lowered their sarissas and upon receiving the order, advanced down the slope.

We see in action on the Macedonian side the Chalkaspides (Bronze Shields) **(1)** believed to form one half or wing, about 8,000 men, of the Antigonid phalanx. Characterized by their bronze shields **(2)**, the *phalangites* are equipped with an assortment of helmets and body armour. As equipment was supplied centrally by the Antigonid state there is, however, a certain amount of uniformity. The comb-crested helmet **(3)**, variously labelled as Thracian or Attic, in particular appears to have been worn by the Antigonid *phalangite*. Body armour in the form of the *linothorax* would also pretty much have been universal. Officers, however, may have worn bespoke helmets and more elaborate body armour. Plumes and crests most likely also denoted officer status **(4)**. The men of the front rank, subject to the greatest danger, were probably equipped with bronze muscle cuirasses **(5)**, which provided added protection.

Opposing the *phalangites* are Roman *hastati*, interspersed with *principes* as the Roman lines are pushed in upon each other **(6)**. Fighting uphill and unable to reach their enemy, they are forced to fall back. The Roman soldiers mostly wear Montefortino helmets and are equipped with a mixture of bronze pectorals **(7)** and iron mail shirts for body armour **(8)**. Some are desperately trying to push aside the wall of pikes or cut off the head of the shafts **(9)**. To no avail, head on and with the advantage of the downhill slope, the pike phalanx is for the moment unassailable.

The Roman counter-attack

Right around this time, the Macedonian left wing had also started to arrive on the ridge but had not yet formed up for battle, with some of its units still making their way up (Polyb.18.25). Having stationed himself on the right, Flamininus now spotted an opportunity. Keeping a cool head amid the carnage and reversal on his left wing, he realized that the enemy left wing was in great disorder, with some units having crested the hill while others were still making their way up. The *phalangites* had also not yet deployed from marching columns into a battle line (Polyb.18.25). It is likely that this part of the Macedonian phalanx consisted of a significant number of new conscripts and were, despite Philip's drilling, still very inexperienced, which may have hampered their ability to carry out the complex manoeuvres now being asked of them.

Flamininus was quick to act. Hoping his crumbling left wing would hold out as long as possible, so as to fix the attention of the imminently victorious Macedonian right, he led the Roman right against the disordered enemy left. The elephants drawn up in front of the *maniples* were sent in first. Their advance proved to be enough to send the disordered Macedonian left flying. There appears to have been a total breakdown in command, chaos reigned, and the phalanx was unable to form up. In these circumstances, the Macedonian soldiers did not hang around to receive the Roman charge but broke in flight. The Romans pursued eagerly and started to run down and slaughter their fleeing enemy (Polyb.18.25–26).

With the Macedonian left suffering total collapse, an unnamed Roman tribune took the initiative to detach 20 *maniples* from the victorious right wing and lead them across the field to the rear of the Macedonian right wing, which had pressed ahead down the slope, rolling up the retreating Roman left. Total disaster now struck Philip, with the Romans suddenly appearing behind his battle line. The tightly packed nature of the Macedonian phalanx did not enable individual soldiers to suddenly face about and defend themselves from

The approximate area where elements of the Macedonian left wing started to deploy. It can be appreciated that the area immediately to their front is slightly broken, potentially making deployment and effective link-up with the advancing right wing difficult. (Photo by Matthew Sears and Jake Butera)

An artist's rendition of the battle of Cynoscephalae depicting the advance of the Macedonian right wing. In reality, the *phalangites* would have been equipped with longer sarissas. (Elbert Perce, public domain, via Wikimedia Commons)

attack from an unexpected direction. More or less powerless to resist, a great many Macedonian soldiers were slain by the onrushing Romans. The *phalangites* at the front would have been unable to gauge clearly what was happening in their rear. They would nonetheless undoubtedly have sensed the terror and slaughter that was breaking up the rear ranks of their formation. Unable to resist this attack from an unexpected direction, Philip's right wing now started to rout; men were throwing away their weapons and tried to make a run for it. Seeing this, the retreating Roman left wing charged in again, adding to the slaughter that now engulfed the Macedonian right (Polyb.18.26).

Philip, meanwhile, had managed to extricate himself from the situation. As soon as he saw the signs of panic and collapse among his men, he retreated with a select body of foot and cavalry to a nearby hill to survey the field. It was now obvious to him that the battle was lost. His right wing, on the verge of victory, had disintegrated under the pressure of the sudden rear attack. His left had not even stood and fought but crumbled upon seeing the enemy elephants approach. Across the field, his men now desperately tried to get away from the onrushing Romans. Seeing that all hope was lost, the king gathered around him as many men as he could and fled as well. Flamininus, meanwhile, was vigorously pursuing the Macedonian left. Cresting the ridge, his men came upon the retreating *phalangites*, who, unable to resist, raised their sarissas upright as a sign of surrender. Having been told this was the customary way of the Macedonians to signal their surrender, the proconsul tried to hold his onrushing men back. In this he was unsuccessful, his vanguard tearing into the stationary enemy and slaughtering many of them, with the survivors throwing away their weapons and fleeing the battlefield (Polyb.18.26).

Total defeat

After pursuing the fleeing Macedonians for a while, the Romans stopped the chase and concentrated on looting the slain and rounding up all the captives. The legionaries also hastened themselves to the enemy camp, expecting rich plunder to be had. They were to be disappointed, however. The Aetolians had got there before them and thoroughly looted the place. This caused a bit of a grumble among the Roman army, who complained to their victorious general that, 'He imposed the dangers upon them, but yielded the spoil to others' (Polyb. 18.27).

The next day, the army rounded up the remaining spoils and marched off towards Larissa, to take control of Philip's base in Thessaly. It left behind 700 of its number, casualties which were presumably mostly incurred by the skirmishing that preceded the battle and subsequently in the fighting between the Macedonian right and Roman left. The forces stationed on the Roman right wing would most likely had incurred little to no casualties, having routed their adversaries before even making contact.

A view from Kremaste looking south towards the plain. The Macedonian right was able to maintain cohesion and utilized the advantage of fighting downhill to push the Roman left back onto the more level ground. (Photo by Robin Waterfield)

Philip, meanwhile, had fled to Gonnoi, where he attempted to collect the survivors of the disaster that had befallen his army. His losses were catastrophic. There had been 8,000 of his men slain in the battle and a further 5,000 more had surrendered (Liv.33.10.7–8); 51 per cent of his army had thus either perished in battle or had been captured by the enemy. Truly devastating losses, although we have to keep in mind that ancient sources are notoriously unreliable when it comes to reporting casualties. The Macedonian right, including the elite royal guard *Agema*, had been crushed between the Roman forces to their front and rear. The heaviest casualties were suffered by these forces during the final phase of the battle when they unexpectedly found the enemy in their rear. The routed Macedonian left suffered severely at the hands of the pursuing Romans, incurring most casualties in the desperate attempt of the *phalangites* to get away from their adversaries. Philip knew he was decisively beaten. Elsewhere his forces had suffered further reverses. The Achaeans defeated his general in a battle outside Corinth and Flamininus' brother Lucius had subdued his remaining ally, Acarnania (Liv.33.15–17). The game was up and Philip knew it. Having taken what remained of his army back to Macedonia, he sent a herald to Flamininus at Larissa, requesting a truce and permission to send an embassy to the senate to start peace negotiations. Despite the strenuous objections of his allies, the Aetolians, who wanted to destroy Philip and the power of the Antigonid monarchy completely, Flamininus granted both requests (Liv.33.11.3–4). After three years, the war had finally come to an end, and with it two centuries of Macedonian domination of Greece.

AFTERMATH

Polybius spends some time musing on the defeat of the Macedonian phalanx by the armies of the Roman Republic, writing:

> As long as the phalanx keeps its own formation and strength no one can resist it in a headlong clash or withstand its charge ... Why is it then that the Romans win, and why are those who use the phalanx defeated? ... It is generally agreed that the phalanx needs ground that is level and open, and which in addition is free from obstacles ... All these are enough to hinder and break up that formation (Polybius 18.28–32).

The battle of Cynoscephalae is not necessarily a clear-cut illustration of this. True, Philip's right wing was caught in the rear and his left wing was unable to deploy effectively or in time to resist the Roman advance, but the phalanx did operate successfully on what is considered to be rough ground. What is more, it succeeded in maintaining its cohesion, advancing down the slope and pushing its Roman adversaries to the brink of collapse. Philip's defeat ultimately resulted from his decision to initiate a full-scale engagement without half of his army being ready and deployed for battle. Against his better judgement, the king had put too much credence in the glowing reports of his officers, and his men paid the price. Defeat in this instance has, therefore, more to do with Philip's generalship and the inability of his left wing, most likely composed of a significant amount of fairly inexperienced recruits, to deploy quickly

Two Roman legionaries and the war god Mars on the altar of Domitius Ahenobarbus. The latter is most probably dressed as a Roman military tribune, wearing muscle cuirass, Etrusco-Corinthian helmet and a cloak. Note the knotted girdle indicating high rank. (Sailko, CC BY-SA 3.0 https://creativecommons.org/licenses/by-sa/3.0, via Wikimedia Commons)

An artist's reconstruction of Flamininus' announcement of Greek 'freedom' at the Isthmian Games in 196 BC. The Roman army left Greece the year after, but would soon return. (Giuseppe Sciuti, public domain, via Wikimedia Commons)

enough rather than intrinsic deficiencies of the phalanx formation itself. The absence of a strategic reserve (akin, for example, to the deployment of the *Agema* by Pyrrhus of Epirus at the battle of Asculum) also prevented the king from responding to developments. This contrasted sharply with the Roman ability to peel off troops from their advancing right wing, wheel them around, and advance against the rear of the advancing Macedonian right. In this context, the inherent inflexibility of the large Macedonian pike blocks versus the manipular legion does play an important role. Once committed and engaged, it was very difficult, but not impossible, for the phalanx to change direction or direct part of the formation to engage an enemy from an unexpected direction. The strength of the formation relied on a single mass of men projecting their pikes and momentum forwards.

Defeated, Philip had to submit himself to the demands of the Roman senate. It was surprisingly lenient, most likely because it had no interest in creating a power vacuum in Greece by doing away with Macedon altogether or enabling the eager Aetolian League to take over. It was also very aware that the other signatory to the 'infamous' pact of kings, Antiochus III, was making his way westward and that a future showdown might be in the offing. Preventing the two kings from joining hands would, therefore, have been a consideration. When peace was signed, Philip was required to give up all his possessions south of Mount Olympus; this included the key fortresses of Demetrias, Chalcis and Acrocorinth. Garrisons from his remaining strongholds in Asia needed to be withdrawn and he was required to hand over the fleet, being allowed to keep only five small warships and one bigger one. On top of this, he was required to pay a large war indemnity. On the plus side, the Antigonid monarchy had not been abolished and Philip was not required to give up his army, which he had already used to good effect to drive out another Dardanian invasion.

Philip V would go on to reign for another 18 years until his death in 179 BC. He put his energies into building up the Macedonian economy and strengthening the recruitment base of his army. His subjects were encouraged to have children, new settlements were founded and Thracians, Gauls and Illyrians were settled in the kingdom. These measures appear to have been highly successful. It allowed his son Perseus to put an army of 43,000 men into the field, which included 29,000 Macedonians. The military resources of the Macedonian state had thus increased significantly in the intervening years. It was precisely this resurgence of Macedonian power, however, and the perceived threat it represented to Rome's interests in the region, that once more would draw the Antigonids and the Roman Republic into conflict and a final confrontation on the field of Pydna.

Having won the battle of Cynoscephalae, Flamininus went on to reorganize the affairs of Greece. Flamininus' Aetolian allies were, however, not amused by the proceedings and were greatly resentful for not having obtained more territorial gains, specifically in Thessaly. They began to agitate against Rome's control of the 'fetters' of Greece, Roman garrisons having taken over from their Antigonid predecessors, claiming that the Greeks appeared to have thrown off the shackles of one master only for them to be replaced by another. After deliberation with the commissioners sent out by the senate, it was decided that a complete withdrawal from Greece by the Roman army offered the best prospects to win over the hearts and minds of the Greeks and cement support for Rome. It would also deny opponents of Rome the opportunity to claim Greece needed liberating. During the Isthmian Games of 196 BC, Flamininus delivered the following proclamation: 'The Senate of Rome and Titus Quinctius the proconsul, after defeating King Philip and the Macedonians, leave the following peoples free, without garrison, without tribute, and in full enjoyment of their ancestral laws: the Corinthians, Phocians, Locrians, Euboeans, Achaeans of Phthiotis, Magnesians, Thessalians, and Perrhaebians' (Polyb.18.46).

In 194 BC, this was followed by a complete withdrawal of the Roman army back to Italy. Back in Rome, Flamininus celebrated a three-day triumph granted in recognition of his achievements. Meanwhile in Greece, smouldering Aetolian resentment against Rome led to the Aetolians inviting Antiochus III over to Greece with an army to liberate the Balkan peninsula from Roman interference. Legion and phalanx were thus gearing up once more to confront each other on the battlefield. Whereas the Second Macedonian War had destroyed the Macedonian hold over mainland Greece, leaving it nominally free but in reality subject to the wishes of Rome, the Syrian War, now about to start, would herald the extension of this policy to the shores of western Asia Minor, marking another key moment in Rome's road to Empire.

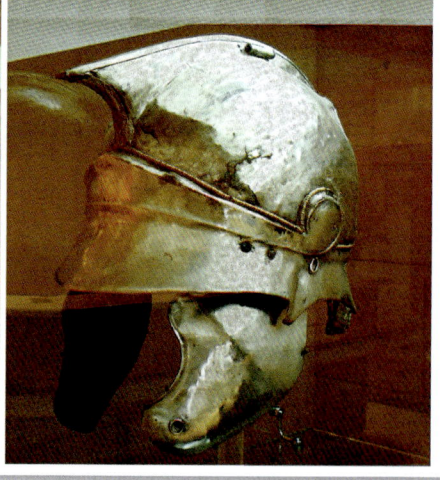

A helmet similar to that depicted on the Aemilius Paulus monument and in the tomb of Lyson and Kalikles. Helmets such as these seem to have been used by Antigonid *phalangites*. (Harrygouvas, CC BY-SA 3.0 https://creativecommons.org/licenses/by-sa/3.0, via Wikimedia Commons)

THE BATTLEFIELD TODAY

As stated, the exact location of the battle of Cynoscephalae is disputed. This study has accepted the location suggested by Hammond that the battle took place on the ridge and spurs separating the modern communities of Zoodochos Pigi and Chalkiades. At the former, he places the Roman camp (having identified its outline while paying a visit to the site) and, at the latter, he has Philip V and the Macedonian army encamped. Both villages can be reached from Pharsalus by taking the Greek national road 3 north, which passes through Chalkiades and close by Zoodochos Pigi. The latter is about 8km from Pharsalus as the crow flies and Chalkiades 12km, so within easy reach of Pharsalus.

Arriving from the direction of Pharsalus, Zoodochos Pigi would be the obvious place to start a tour of the battlefield. With Hammond's map in hand, the visitor would be able to identify the area where the Roman army would have encamped and drawn up for battle. Of particular note are the ruined remains of a church and cemetery close to where Hammond identified the remains of a Roman camp. A recent exploration of the site by Butera and Sears (2019) was able to observe the markings identified by Hammond as well. Their excellent chapter about the battle of Cynoscephalae in their *Battles and Battlefields of Ancient Greece* comes highly recommended and will be indispensable to any visitor of the site, providing guidance as it does about how best to explore the battlefield.

Gazing north, the Kremaste Spur and ridge, over which the initial skirmishes were fought and down whose slope Philip charged, are easily identifiable. Local unmade roads lead north towards the Kremaste Spur with its tiny hamlet and the ridge beyond. In between lie the flatter areas identified by Hammond onto which the Roman left wing was pushed back. Looking east, one is able to identify the spur across which the Roman right wing advanced onto the ridge routing the Macedonian left. Doubling back to Zoodochos Pigi and national road 3, one can drive up to Chalkiades and nearby Ano Chalkiades. From here, local roads give access to the ridge separating the two armies and the Kremaste Spur. The high point of the ridge is marked by a concrete water reservoir, which possibly denotes the boundary between the deployment of the Macedonian right and left. The latter would have attempted to deploy to the south-west of this feature, whereas Philip himself and the right wing would have advanced down the spur.

The supposed site of the Roman camp near Zoodochos Pigi. The faint lines visible on the ground have been identified as the outlines of part of a Roman camp. (Photo by Matthew Sears and Jake Butera)

BIBLIOGRAPHY

Primary sources

Appian (trans. H. White), *The Foreign Wars*, New York: The Macmillan Company (1899)

Cassius Dio (trans. E. Cary, and H. B. Forster), *Roman History, Volume VII: Books 56–60*, Loeb Classical Library 175, Cambridge, MA: Harvard University Press (1924)

Diodorus Siculus (trans. F. R. Walton), *Library of History, Volume XI: Fragments of Books 21–32*, Loeb Classical Library 409, Cambridge, MA: Harvard University Press (1957)

Marcus Junianus Justinus (trans. J. S. Watson), *Epitome of the Philippic History of Pompeius Trogus*, London: Henry G. Bohn, York Street, Convent Garden (1853)

Livy (trans. W. M. Roberts), *History of Rome*, New York: E. P. Dutton and Co. (1912)

Livy (trans. E. T. Sage), *The History of Rome, Books XXXI–XXXIV*, Cambridge, MA, London: Harvard University Press: Heinemann (1935)

Livy (trans. J. C. Yardley), *History of Rome, Volume IX: Books 31–34*, Loeb Classical Library 295. Cambridge, MA: Harvard University Press, (2017)

Plutarch (trans. B. Perrin), *Lives, Volume X: Agis and Cleomenes. Tiberius and Gaius Gracchus. Philopoemen and Flamininus*, Loeb Classical Library 102, Cambridge, MA: Harvard University Press (1921)

Polyaenus (trans. R. Shepherd), *Stratagems of War*, Chicago: Ares (1793: reprinted Chicago, 1974)

Polybius (trans. E. S. Shuckburg), *Histories*, London, New York: Macmillan (1889, reprint Bloomington 1962)

Polybius (trans. W. R. Paton. Revised by F. W. Walbank, Christian Habicht), *The Histories, Volume V: Books 16–27*, Loeb Classical Library 160. Cambridge, MA: Harvard University Press (2012)

Secondary sources

Butera, C. J., and Sears, M. A., *Battles and Battlefields of Ancient Greece: A Guide to Their History, Topography and Archaeology*, Yorkshire: Pen and Sword Military (2019)

Charles, M. B. and Rhodan, P., '"Magister Elephantorvm": A Reappraisal of Hannibal's Use of Elephants', *Classical World* 100(4): 363–89 (2007)

Cole, M., *Legion Versus Phalanx: The Epic Struggle for Infantry Supremacy in the Ancient World*, Oxford: Osprey Publishing (2020)

D'Amato, R., *Republican Roman Warships 509–27 BC*, Oxford: Osprey Publishing (New Vanguard 225) (2015)

Dean, S., 'Equipment of the Macedonian Wars, Pilum vs Pike', *Ancient Warfare* VIII: 37–42 (2014)

Dell, H. J., 'The origin and nature of Illyrian piracy', *Historia: Zeitschrift für Alte Geschichte* 16: 344–58 (1967)

Du Plessis, J. C., '"Synaspismos" and its possibility in the Macedonian Styled Phalanx', *Akropolis* 3(1): 167–83 (2019)

Du Plessis, J. C., *The Seleucid Army of Antiochus the Great: Weapons, Armour and Tactics*, Barnsley: Pen and Sword Military (2022)

Eckstein, A. M., 'The Pact between the Kings, Polybius 15.20.6, and Polybius' View of the Outbreak of the Second Macedonian War', *Classical Philology* 100(3): 228–42 (2005)

Eckstein, A. M., *Rome Enters the Greek East: From Anarchy to Hierarchy in the Hellenistic Mediterranean, 230–170 BC*, Chichester: Wiley-Blackwell (2012)

Errington, R. M., 'Rome against Philip and Antiochus', in A. E. Astin, F. W. Walbank, M. W. Frederiksen, R. M. Ogilvie (eds), *The Cambridge Ancient History VIII, Rome and the Mediterranean to 133 B.C.*, Cambridge University Press: 244–89 (1989)

Errington, R. M., *A History of the Hellenistic World*, Malden, MA: Blackwell Publishing (2008)

Errington, R. M., and Errington, C., *A History of Macedonia*, Oxford: University of California Press (1990)

Fields, N. and Anderson, D., *The Roman Army of the Punic Wars, 264–146 BC*, Oxford: Osprey Publishing (Battle Orders 27) (2007)

Fields, N., *Roman Republican Legionary 298–105 BC*, Oxford: Osprey Publishing (Warrior 162) (2012)

Gaebel, R. E., *Cavalry Operations in the Ancient Greek World*, Norman: University of Oklahoma Press (2002)

Gowers, W., 'The African elephant in warfare', *African Affairs* 46(182): 42–49 (1947)

Hammond, N. G., 'The opening campaigns and the battle of the Aoi Stena in the Second Macedonian War', *The Journal of Roman Studies* 56(1–2): 39–54 (1966)

Hammond, N. G., 'The campaign and the battle of Cynoscephalae in 197 BC', *The Journal of Hellenic Studies* 108: 60–82 (1988)

Hammond, N. G., Griffith, G. T. and Walbank, F. W., *A History of Macedonia: 336–167 BC (Vol. 3)*, Oxford: Oxford University Press (1972)

Hatzopoulos, M. B. and Juhel, P., 'Four Hellenistic Funerary Stelae from Gephyra, Macedonia', *American Journal of Archaeology* 113: 423–37 (2009)

Head, D. and Heath, I., *Armies of the Macedonian and Punic Wars 359 BC to 146 BC: Organization, Tactics, Dress and Weapons*, Goring-by-Sea: Wargames Research Group (1982)

Heckel, W. and Jones, R., *Macedonian Warrior: Alexander's Elite Infantryman*, Oxford: Osprey Publishing (Warrior 103) (2006)

Johstono, P. A., *Military Institutions and State Formation in the Hellenistic Kingdoms*, Doctoral dissertation, Duke University (2012)

Juhel, P. and Sekunda, N. V., 'The agema and "the other Peltasts" in the late Antigonid Army, and in the Drama/Cassandreia Conscription diagramma', *Zeitschrift für Papyrologie und Epigraphik* 170: 104–08 (2009)

Karunanithy, D., *The Macedonian War Machine: Neglected Aspects of the Armies of Philip, Alexander and the Successors (359-281 BC)*, Barnsley: Pen and Sword Military (2013)

Livingston, M. and Cole, M., 'Finding Cynoscephalae – 197 BC, Sources to Results', *Ancient Warfare* IX(6): 8–15 (2015)

Ma, J., 'The Attalids: A Military History', in P. Thonemann (ed.), *Attalid Asia Minor: Money, International Relations and the State*, Oxford: Oxford University Press: 49–82 (2013)

Matthew, C., *An Invincible Beast: Understanding the Hellenistic Pike-Phalanx in Action*, Barnsley: Pen and Sword Military (2015)

Matyszak, Philip, *Roman Conquests: Macedonia and Greece*, Barnsley: Pen and Sword Military (2009)

McDonald A. H. and Walbank F. W., 'The Origins of the Second Macedonian War', *Journal of Roman Studies* 27(2): 180–207 (1937)

McDonnel-Staff, P., 'Sparta's last hurrah, the battle of Sellasia (222 BC)', *Ancient Warfare* II(2): 23–29 (2008)

McDonnel-Staff, P., 'Macedon's Last Hurrah – The Third Macedonian War and Pydna', *Ancient Warfare* IV(6): 33–37 (2010)

McDonnel-Staff, P., 'The elite guard infantry of the Antigonid Macedonian army, Hypaspists to Peltasts', *Ancient Warfare* V(6): 20–25 (2011)

Mihajlov, A. R., *Greek Riders of War: Cavalrymen of Ancient Greece*, Doctoral dissertation, University of Auckland (2018)

Morton, J. N., *Shifting Landscapes, Policies, and Morals: A Topographically Driven Analysis of the Roman Wars in Greece from 200 BC to 168 BC*, Doctoral dissertation, University of Pennsylvania (2017)

Nefedkin, A. K., 'On the origin of Greek cavalry shields in the Hellenistic period', *Klio* 91(2): 356–66 (2009)

Neumann, C., 'A Note on Alexander's March-Rates', *Historia: Zeitschrift für Alte Geschichte* 20(2/3): 196–98 (1971)

Nutt, S. W., *Tactical Interaction and Integration: A Study in Warfare in the Hellenistic Period from Philip II to the Battle of Pydna*, Doctoral Thesis, Newcastle University (1993)

O'Neil, J. L., 'The Ethnic Origins of the Friends of the Antigonid Kings of Macedon', *The Classical Quarterly* 53(2): 510–22 (2003)

Park, M., 'The battle of Cynoscephalae, 197 BC, the Dogs' Heads', *Ancient Warfare* VIII: 25–32 (2014)

Post, R., 'Bright colours and uniformity, Hellenistic military costume', *Ancient Warfare* IV(6): 14–19 (2010)

Roisman, J. and Worthington, I., *A Companion to Ancient Macedonia*, Malden: Wiley-Blackwell (2010)

Rzepka, J., *The Aetolian Elite Warriors and Fifth-Century Roots of Hellenistic Confederacy*, Warszawa: Instytut Historyczny UW (2009)

Sage, Michael M., *The Army of the Roman Republic: From the Regal Period to the Army of Julius Caesar*, Pen and Sword Military (2018)

Sekunda, N., *Republican Roman Army 200–104 BC*, Oxford: Osprey Publishing (1996)

Sekunda, N., 'The Macedonian Army', in J. Roisman and I. Worthington (eds), *A Companion to Ancient Macedonia*, Malden: Wiley-Blackwell: 446–71 (2010)

Sekunda, N., 'Cavalry, Hellenistic', *The Encyclopedia of Ancient History* (2012)

Sekunda, N., *Macedonian Armies after Alexander 323–168 BC*, Oxford: Osprey Publishing (Men-at-Arms 477) (2012)

Sekunda, N., *The Antigonid Army (No. 8)*, Gdańsk: Akanthina (2013)

Sekunda, N., *The Army of Pyrrhus of Epirus*, Oxford: Osprey Publishing (Men-at-Arms 528) (2019)

Sekunda N., and de Souza P., 'Military forces', in P. Sabin, H. van Wees and M. Whitby (eds), *The Cambridge History of Greek and Roman Warfare*, Cambridge University Press: 325–67 (2007)

Skarmintzos, S., 'Phalanx versus Legion, Greco-Roman conflict in the Hellenistic era', *Ancient Warfare* II(2): 30–34 (2008)

Strootman, R., 'Alexander's Thessalian cavalry', *Talanta* 42/43: 51–67 (2012)

Taylor, M. J., 'Roman infantry tactics in the mid-Republic: a reassessment', *Historia: Zeitschrift für Alte Geschichte* 63: 301–22 (2014)

Taylor, M. J., 'The battle scene on Aemilius Paullus' Pydna monument: a reevaluation', *Hesperia: The Journal of the American School of Classical Studies at Athens* 85(3): 559–76 (2016)

Taylor, R., *The Macedonian Phalanx: Equipment, Organization and Tactics from Philip and Alexander to the Roman Conquest*, Havertown: Pen and Sword (2020)

Thiel, J. H., *Studies on the History of Roman Sea-Power in Republican Times*, Amsterdam: North-Holland Publishing Co. (1946)

Walbank, F. W., *Philip V of Macedon, The Hare Prize Essay 1939*, Cambridge: Cambridge University Press (1940)

Warry. J., *Warfare in the Classical World: An Illustrated Encyclopedia of Weapons, Warriors and Warfare in the Ancient Civilisations of Greece and Rome*, Salamander Books Ltd (1980)

Waterfield, R., *Taken at the Flood: The Roman Conquest of Greece*, Oxford: Oxford University Press (2014)

Webber, C., 'Fighting on all sides, Thracian mercenaries of the Hellenistic Era', *Ancient Warfare* IV(6): 38–43 (2010)

Worthington, I., *The Last Kings of Macedonia and the Triumph of Rome*, New York: Oxford University Press (2023)

INDEX

Figures in bold refer to illustrations.

Acarnanian League 13, 87
Achaea 15, 25, 26, 38, 39, 64–65, 87
Aetolia and the Macedonian Wars 9, 10, 15, 18, 25, 51, **52**, 58, 64, 66, **68**, 69, 70, 76, 86, 87, 90
Aetolian army 26
  epilektoi 26
Aetolian league 7–8, 10, 40
Agron, King (Illyria) 6
Alexander the Great (Macedon) 5, **5**, 31
altar of Domitius Ahenobarbus **22**, **23**, **25**, 88
Amynander, King (Athamania) 17, 18, 40, 51, 58, 70
Antigonid Macedonian army 5, 9, **13**, 19, 27, **27**–32, **28**, **32**, 37, **38**, 43, 44, 56, 57, 58, 67, **68**, 71, 73, **74**–**75**, 76, **78**–**79**, 80, **80**, 85, **85**, 87, **89**, 91
  auxiliaries and mercenaries 27, 32, 53, 81
    Thracian mercenaries **60**–**61**, 62, 66
  cavalry 31, 38, 44, 45, **45**, **46**–**47**, 48, 49, **49**, 50, 51
    Thessalian cavalry 31–32
  Chalkaspides (Bronze Shields) 29, 30, 32, 49, **82**–**83**, 84
  hypaspistai (elite infantry) 5
  Leukaspides (White Shields) 29
  peltasts 30, 36, 44, **60**–**61**, **62**, 63, 66
    Agema (elite royal guard) 30–31, 44–45, 77, 87, 89
    phalangites 27–28, 29, 30, **41**, 54, 63, 66, **75**, 79, **82**–**83**, 84, 85, 86, 86, 87, **90**
Antigonus II Gonatus, King (Macedon) 6, 9, 27
Antigonus III Doson, King (Macedon) 7, 18, 27
Antiochus III, Seleucid Emperor 10, **11**, 13, 14, 15, 16, 17, 18, 19, 89, 90
Apollonia, Illyria 7, 9, 14, 15
Apustius, Lucius 16, 33, 39, 40, 42, 50, 55, 65
Argead royal line 5
Aristaenus 64–65
armour and equipment **22**, **23**, **25**, 28, 30, 44, **46**–**47**, 48, 54, 56, **82**–**83**, 84
  linothorax (linen armour) 27, 28, **32**, 38, 39, **46**–**47**, 48, 84
  shields 28, 31, **31**, 32, **46**–**47**, 48, 49, 55, **60**–**61**, 62
    scutum (body shield) 22, **23**
    thureos (shield) 26, **26**, 29, 32, **39**, **60**–**61**, 62
Athamanian army 59
Athenagoras 19, 40, 44, 45, 50, 53, 76
Athens 13–14, 33, 36–39
Attalus I, King (Pergamon) 9, 10, 11, 14, 17, **18**, 50, 66, 67

Attica 13, 19, 33, 35, 36, 38, 39, 40

Barca, Hannibal 10, 11, 13, 17, 19
Bato, King (Dardania) 40
Battle for Atrax (198 BC) 15
Battle for the Aous gorge (198 BC) 15, 19, 27, **52**, 53–54, 55, 56–59, **57**, 58, **60**–**61**, **62**, 65
battle formations **22**–**23**, **24**–**25**, 26, 45, 54
  Macedonian pike phalanx 27–30, **28**, 31, 33, 56, 63, 67, 73, **73**, **74**, 75, 77, 80, **80**, 81, **82**–**83**, 84, 85–86, 88, 89
  rhomboid 31
  testudo 50, 63
  triplex acies **22**, **23**, 24
Battle of Cannae (216 BC) 8
Battle of Çërravë/Otolobus (199 BC) 44–49, **46**–**47**, 48, 51
Battle of Chalcis (200 BC) 16, **35**, 35–36, 38
Battle of Chios (201 BC) 11–12, 13
Battle of Cynoscephalae (197 BC) 19, 20, 26, 27, 31, 67–70, **68**, **73**, 73–87, **74**–**75**, 76, **78**–**79**, 80, 81, **82**–**83**, 84, 85, 86, 87, 88, 91, 92
Battle of Ilipa (206 BC) 15
Battle of Lake Trasimene (217 BC), 15 8
Battle of Magnesia (190 BC) 29, 39
Battle of Zama (202 BC) 13, 15, 21, **21**
Boeotia 15, 64, 66, 69
Boeotian League 67
Bol, Ferdinand 8
bribery 40

campaign of 198 BC **52**
campaigning season 33, 34, 39, 59, 66
Carthage 8, 9, 21, 25
Carthaginian army 21
Cento, Claudius 33, 35
Cento, Gaius Claudius 16
Cleopatra VII, Queen (Egypt) 5
coin portraits 17, **18**, 31, **45**, 48
conferences for negotiated peace settlements 55, **57**, 65–66, 67, 87, 89
Cretan army 25, 26, 44, 45
  archers 32, **46**–**47**, 48

Damocritus 40
Dardanian invasions of Macedonia 49, 50, 51, 53, 89
deaths 9, 12, 35, 37, 39, 40, 43, 45, 49, 56, 80, 81, 86, 87
Demetrius of Pharos 6, 7, 8, 9
deserters 43
dynastic rivalries and disputes 5, 19

Epirote League 58
Epirus 55, 58
Euboea 51

Fabritius (Roman consul) 8
first battle of Velestino (1897) **71**
First Illyrian War (229 BC) 6, 15
First Macedonian War (214–205 BC) 8–10, 13, 16, **18**, 26, 36
Flamininus, Lucius Quinctius 17, 20, 55, 65, 87
Flamininus, Titus Quinctius 15, **16**, 16–17, **17**, 20, 32, **52**, 54–55, 56, **57**, 58–63, **63**, 64, **64**, 65, 66, **66**, 67, **68**, 69, 70, 72, **72**, 73, **75**, 76, 77, **78**–**79**, 80, 85, 86, 87, **89**, 90
foraging 38, **42**, 44, 45, 48, **75**, 77

Galba, Publius Sulpicius 15, 16, 20, 25, 33, 40, 41, **43**, 44, 45, 49, 50, 54, 58, 77
Galba, Servius Sulpicius 16
Genusus river valley 43

Hellenic Security Pact 7, 8, 13, 34, 58
helmets 13, 14, 28, 30, 32, 43, 45, 49, **60**–**61**, 62, 90
  Boeotian 25, 38, **46**–**47**, 48
  Etrusco-Corinthian **22**, **23**, 88
  konos/pinos 28, 39, **46**–**47**, 48, 54
  Montefortino **21**, **22**, **24**, **82**–**83**, 84
  Phrygian **60**–**61**, 62
  Thracian/Attic 28, **82**–**83**, 84
Heracleides of Gyrton 19, 41
hoplites 22, 26, **26**
House of Menander, Pompeii 36

Illyrian kingdom 6, 8, 9, 10, 12, 15, 19, 33, 40
intelligence 9, 43
Isthmian Games 15, **89**, 90

Khlidi Pass **42**
Kremaste Spur **74**–**75**, 76, 79, 80, 81, 87, 91

Laevinus, Marcus Valerius 9
lembi (ships) 8, 9, **9**, 11, 12, 26
Leon 19
Lepidus, Marcus Aemilius 14
Livius, Titus 5
Livy 22, 26, 31, 35, 36, 37, 41, 43, 44, 45, 49, 53, 56, 59, 63, 71, 72, 73
logistics and supplies 12, 20, 41, 44, 45, 50, 51, 53, 58–63, **63**, 64, **64**, 67, 69, 71
Lyson and Kallikles tomb 32

Macedon allies 7, 64–65, 67, 69, 87
Macedon dominance 6, 7, **12**, 90
Macedonian navy 8, 9, 11, 12, **18**, 34, 50, **50**, 89
Macedonian–Seleucid pact 13, 15
Macedonian strategy 7, 7, 8–11, 12–13, 14, 15, 18–19, **19**, 27, 34, 36–39,

95

40–41, **42**, 43–45, 49–50, 51, **52**, 53, 54, 55, 58, 63, 64–65, 67–69, **68, 69**, 70, 71–73, **75**, 76, 77–80, 81, 85–86, **87**, 88–89
maniples and legions 22–23, 24, **60–61, 62**, 78–79, 80–81, 85
matèriel losses 12, 36
mercenaries 19, 26, 27, 32, 37, 45, **60–61, 62**, 66, **75**, 76, 79
military strengths and complements 11, 20–21, 22, 23, 26, 27, 28–29, 31, 36, 38, 41, 43, 44–45, 54, 55, 66, 71, **75**, **79**, 89
Monophthalmos, Antigonus 5
morale and discipline 9, 43, 44, 45, 50, 56, 64

Nabis, King (Sparta) 19, 38
Nicanor 14, 19, 75, 77, 80
Nicomedes II, King (Bithynia) **31**

peace of Phoinike (205 BC) 10, 15
Pergamon and the Pergamenes 10, 11, **11**, 12, **12**, 13, 14, 15, 25, 26, 37
Pergamon navy 26
Perseus 40, 43, 89
Persian Empire 5
Philip II, King (Macedon) 31
Philip V, King (Macedon) 6–7, 7, 8, 8–9, 9, 10, 11, 12, 13, 14, 15, 16, **16**, 18, 18–19, **19**, 27, 31, 32, 34, 36, 37, 37–39, 40, 41, **42**, 43–44, 45, 46–47, **48**, 49, 50, 51, **52**, 53, 55, 56, 58, 63, 64–66, **67**, 67–69, **68, 69**, 70, 71–73, **73**, 74, **75**, 76, 77–80, 79, 81, 84, 86, 87, 88, 89
Philocles 19, 38, 39
Pleuratus, King (Ardiaei tribe) 40
Plutarch 32, 54, 55, 59
political ambitions 17
Polybius 5, 8, 11, 22, 31, 71, 72, 77, 88
Pompey the Great 5
port of Anticyra, Phocis 64, **64**, 66
Ptolemy 5
Pyrrhus, King (Epirus) **8**, 13, 31, 89

reconnaissance and scouting 36, 59, 70, 73–76, **75**
recruitment and military service 23, 24, 27, 89
reinforcements and reserves 20, 21, 37, 39, 51, 66, 69, 75, 76, 89
Rhodes 10–11, 13, 14, **18**, 25
Rhodian navy **11**, 11–12, 26
Roman allies 15, 18, 24–25, 40, **43**, 51, 64–65, 90
Roman army 20, 37, 40–41, **42**, 43, 45, 57, 58, 65, 68, 70, 71, 72, **73**, 74–75, 78–79, 80, 80–81, **81**, 86, 88, 89, 90, 91, **91**
  auxiliaries 20
  Greek 25–26
  equites (cavalry) 22, **46–47, 48**, 49, 56
  hastati (young men) 22, 23, **60–61, 62**, 82–83, 84
  legions 21, 22–23, 24–25
  principes (older men) 22, 23, **82–83**, 84
  triarii (older veterans) 22, 23
  velites 22, **60–61, 62**, 74
Roman campaign of 200–199 BC 40–51, **42, 43, 46–47, 48**
Roman consulship 16, 17, 54
Roman navy 9, 20, 26, 35, 38, 40, **50**, 65
Roman–Rhodian–Pergamene naval alliance 17, 40, 50, **50**, 51
Roman Republic and Empire 5–6, **6**, 11, 13, 16, 19, 90
Roman senate 66, 89, 90
Roman strategy 6, **6**, 8, 9, 10, 11, **11**, 13–14, 15, 16, 20, 26, 33, 35–36, 39–40, 41, **42**, 44, 45, 50, 54–55, 56, **57**, 58–64, **64**, 65, 66, 67, 69, 70, 71, 72, 73–76, **74**, 77, 78, 79, 80–85, 86, 89

Sacred Squadrons **46–47**, 48
Scipio 55
Second Illyrian War (219 BC) 6, 15
Second Macedonian War (200–197 BC) 15, 16, 20, 21, 24, 25, 26, 90

Second Punic War (201 BC) 15, 21, 23, 24, 25
Seleucid Empire 10, 12, **12**, 13, 17
siege of Atrax (198 BC) 63, 69, 81
siege of Elateia (198 BC) **52**, 64, 65
siege of Thaumaci (199 BC) 51
skirmishing tactics 26, 31
Social War (220–217 BC) 7, 15, 18, 34
Sparta 17, 19

temple of Diana 7
terrain factors 30, 32, 50, 56, 69, 70, 71, **71**, 73, 76, 77, 81, **81**
Teuta, Queen (Illyria) 6, **6**
Thebes, Boeotia 66, 67, 70, 71

Thessaly 7, 9, 10, 15, 40, **42**, 51, 52, 55, 58–59, 64, 65, 66, 67, 69, 86, 90
Thessaly campaign 59
Thetideum sanctuary at Zoodochos Pigi 72, **72**
thureophoroi (Greek infantry) 26, **26**, 32, 43
training and experience 23–24, 27, 67, **67**, 85, 88

Villius Tappulus, Publius 16, 17, 41, 54

war booty 36, 58, 86
war elephants 21, 25, 41, 45, 77, 78–79, 80, 85
war indemnity payments 89
weaponry 22, 25, 31, 39, 43, 44, 54
  catapults 56, 57
  gladius Hispaniensis (sword) 22, 24, 44, **46–47, 48, 60–61**, 62
  javelins 22, 31, **60–61**, 62
  pila (spears) 22, 23, 26, **26**, 30, **46–47, 48**, 50, 63
  rhomphaia 32, **62**
  sarissas (pikes) 26, 27–28, **28**, 30, 33, 50, 81, 86, **86**, 89
weather conditions 33, 73, 76